DISTORTED VIEW

My Life, My Journey

Cherelle Patrice Ward
Author

Cherelle Patrice Ward
www.http//cpatrice.net/
Uncover@newimageministry.com
Info@cpatrice.net

Cover design by Carl D. Wright
www.carldwright.com

Book layout by Amber Mabry
www.ambermabrythrives.com

ISBN – Paperback
979-8-9890175-0-8

First Edition: 2023
Consultant – Gail E. Dudley
www.GailDudley.com

CONTENTS

FOREWORD

I have had the privilege of being a senior pastor in the African American Church experience for 33 years. For thirty-one of those years, I have had the blessing of that position being my sole and or primary source of income. Full-time pastoral ministry gives the pastor a vivid view into the lives of the many people he/she may lead.

What I have found over these three decades is that from generation to generation the issues remain the same that the people of God are trying their best to navigate. Education, employment, health, relationships, finances, family, and faith are all at the top of the list for everyone, male and female alike.

However, I have also found that this list is usually much more challenging for those who are female. It would be disingenuous at the very least to present these very genuine issues as equal between both male and female. In my experience every one of the issues listed above become more challenging if you are a woman. We do not like to admit it. We are just getting to the place of talking about it, but the landscape of life favors the masculine at almost every turn.

This is not just in society; this is also true when we are speaking of what is supposed to be the safety and sanctity of the home.

This perpetual uphill journey and uneven playing field has caused women to second guess themselves, yes, even doubt themselves in education, employment, health, relationships, finances, family, and faith. A plethora of women endure these struggles for a lifetime because somehow to reject the struggle or to desire more makes you less of a woman.

Women receive defining adjectives like angry, difficult, mean, ungrateful, ugly, disrespectful, and selfish to name a few. To hear it over and over again is to produce cases of self-fulfilling prophecy in the life or lives of the women who hear it.

From that place she will spend years trying to live a life that pleases the people who will never find it in their hearts to give a passing grade for existence in life. If she is not conforming to the agenda of others, she is not fulfilling her role as a valuable human.

These sentiments have produced brokenness, depression, and even suicidal ideations that can haunt women for a lifetime. Couple this with things like negative body imaging, ageism, sexism, and racism the life of any woman can become nothing more than a well-dressed and decorated prison.

This is why we need to celebrate, endorse, and promote a work like *Distorted View*. Cherelle Patrice Ward in this works unlocks the potential release of not just every woman that will read it, but every person.

Distorted View is a very brave and candid disclosure of how so many of us can become trapped by the opinions and plans of others and waste years trying to satisfy a bar that continuously moves and changes. Cherelle is living proof that distorted views can become views that are vividly clear because we give ourselves the time and space to recover and to simply be.

I am excited for any person who will dare take the journey and correct their distorted view of themselves and the others who ushered them into such a hellish place to begin with.
Read It and Be Renewed....

Bishop Kenneth W. Paramore, D.Min.

INTRODUCTION

I have often viewed a happy life as simple, loving, and stable, with family, close friends, a mother, and father living happily ever after. In this fairytale depiction of a life, I believed this would happen for me as I became an adult. This was my very real image in my mind. If you loved God and did good you would have good done to you, whatever you put out in life would be what is returned to you. However, what we view may not always be actual, it may not be in our vision at all. That often left me with a distorted view or a distorted self-image. You may ask how can I say that? I cannot about every person's view, however, I can say that about mine.

As a child I grew to love carnivals and amusement parks every summer my father would take our family. I remember going to a local carnival and getting a chance to walk through this fun house of mirrors, I was amazed! It was funny to me how every mirror in that house made me look a different way, distorted even, a big head with a skinny body, or big body and a little head, all out of shape, it was fun and exciting to see myself in various ways, never knowing that the very fun house vision of myself would creep into the reality of my life.

As a child I was always taught to be kind and sweet and respect others, love, and respect God and love your family; I took those directives literally and I exercised it so much so that it truly is a part of who I am. I have always tried to be a good person and never cause any trouble, trusting everyone who is supposed to love me and care for me, until life happened, and I did not anymore.

CHAPTER 1 MEAGER BEGINNINGS

Let me introduce you to my life, I was born in the month of June 1966; I made my arrival earlier than intended, a few months early. Born a preemie 2lbs 6 ounces and everyone was praying I make it at such an early stage. I was hospitalized for months before I could be released to my young parents, my mother 16 years of age and my father 19 years of age, they married after finding out they were expecting a child. Back then that is what they would call a shotgun wedding if you will!

It was quick, my mother was all of 98 pounds and 5 months pregnant, and my father was fresh out of high school and working. The hospital staff and most people did not believe I would even make it since I was so little, not developed and about 4 months early, my chances back then were slim to none. But look at what the prayers and Gods hand over my life did! I made it! So, there is no doubt in my mind that there is purpose in my being here on this earth.

I am the eldest of all my siblings, my mother and father had 5 girls together, and some years later my father remarried and began a new family, there came 2 boys and another girl. So, then I became the eldest of 8. My age made a huge difference in feeling like part of my younger sibling's life, for I had children about the same age as they were, perhaps dynamics played a huge role too, my sisters and I were literally the Jackson 5 for almost 30 years by the time the additional 3 came, my sisters and I were all grown with families of our own.

The sibling relationship between myself and the younger children was never real close for me, I know who they are and love them, they are my siblings, but the age difference and life situations never grew the relationships into what my sisters and I have, clearly that was to be expected.

One thing about my childhood I don't believe many know is I loved fantasy, and still do to some degree, especially in watching movies however, I have had to learn to accept the fact that not all that looks like a diamond is in fact a diamond at all, and not all that looks like the happy home with the white picket fence, perfect kids, a mother and a father living happily ever after may not be happy at all; as well as a playful comment may not be playful at all, in fact it can be a underlined degrading thought, and an innocent touch is not so innocent especially when you are a child, and you love the relative you that tells you to never tell anyone. Yes, I loved fantasy so much because it was always a good place and happiness ever after was something I deeply believed would be for me. I remember one summer day at one of the many family reunions picnic my father's side of the family had. My grandmother, the mother of my father, was huge on the family coming together at least once a year, and they were large so much so that everyone came to our reunions even if they were not family by blood but family by friendship and relationship.

That day I remember my father saying to me in a very stern voice, "Cherelle, everyone is not going to like you! Or be like you! and they won't do for you, what you would do for them" this comment came after he heard one of my cousins saying a derogatory statement to me, just so happens my father was watching and listening from a near distance, sadly once my cousins' statement was over, I was not upset or even the lease bit hurt because I took it as a playful gesture, however, my father did not! He told me at once do not ever let anyone call you what you are not! You must stop letting people say mean things to you, and stop being so timid! I was 12 years old at that time, I told him "Dad, they always call me that, it's just playing around."

At the time I did not understand why my father was so upset when he heard the statement and saw how I reacted to it. I learned later in life exactly what my dad meant about my passive behavior and allowing negative comments to be spoken to me repeatedly, that repeated behavior can manifest that very thought within you, you will believe just what others say about you and to you.

As always, I wanted to view everything about life as great and wonderful so I took a lot of derogatory statements from people that I never should have. Throughout my life circumstances and life issues that was one of the reasons that caused me to see myself with a distorted view. In this book you will travel the journey of me but before we move forward let me encourage you to read this with your eyes open wide without distorted films causing you to see past what reality is and only see what was superficial.

CHAPTER 2 FALSE TRUTHS

I will confess and praise you, for you are fearful and wonderful; and for the awful wonder of my birth! AMP PSALMS 139:14a [1]

Before you begin to judge this chapter's title, my false truth, have you always been honest with yourself? Are you living in your truth after a life of covering up the real places we keep hidden? If not, please take your mask off to fully understand and see what I will share in this chapter. I am going to be transparent here and let you know my life was a lie! Yes, I said it, my life was a lie and here is why it was a lie.

I lived my life from as far back as I can remember until the age of about 46 years old, having a mask on internally to cover the external. I have lived a lot of years making myself look like I had it all together nothing bothering me, and nothing going to stop me from being Cherelle the good one, the kind one and the one who has a good relationship with everyone even when I was hurting, sad unhappy and downright miserable. I have seen myself through the mirror of distortion for many years, too many years, decades even. Losses, disappointments, shame, embarrassment, low self-esteem, failures, lack of self-care and mental anguish shaped the view of who I saw daily. I will say I am no longer ashamed of who I am, I have come to a place of acceptance and realize that I made some mistakes in my life, **but I realize that my life was never a mistake.**

I quoted the scripture above in Psalms, it speaks of giving thanks for being fearfully and wonderfully made, if you do not know, I was born and raised in the church. Grew up in a Christian family and home. I have only known my dad to be one of the greatest preachers on this side of heaven! And I mean that from deep within, he was a quiet storm if you will. So, to give God praise was easy especially as a child for me I was taught how to do that, I started as young as 2 years old singing and praising God in church.

I had a relationship with God from an early age and as I grew into my tween and teen years that relationship grew. I went to church; I love God and praised like all the other young people on Sundays, I was a respectful daughter and kind person and found out that secrets are to be kept so you will not hurt anyone else, but what is done in the dark always seems to come to light. Remember I am telling this from how I was viewing me, so just hold on to your comments. I was teased a lot as a kid, I had 4 eyes and could not see a thing without those big glasses, I had a big nose, and big lips with big feet that looked like my dad's.

I never saw myself as the dainty one with small features like my sisters. I felt like the odd one, so I aways made up for it by trying to be good, never crossing the line to do wrong, always following directives. So praising was in my DNA thinking was wonderful and fearfully made I never thought it at all. You see the comments and laughs of being the ugly one was embedded in me, I began to think that I was what they called me, this was the beginning of my distorted view.

Have you ever lived with a negative view of yourself? Have you ever believed that you will never be more than what you have been told? I'll tell you it is possible because that is what I experienced, when you are young you tend to trust and believe in those who are to love you, care for you and protect you, I have experienced a time in my young life that left an impression no child should have to live with, the trauma of sexual assault can leave a lasting impression on a person's psyche and self-worth.

I spoke in the introduction of an innocent touch may not be innocent at all. The perpetrator may have never thought any damage would be done at all, but it did, a seed of promiscuity was planted, as a child I didn't know exactly what was happening, but it left a horrible stench in my nostrils and a life of hiding to cover the actions of one who really didn't care at all, it wasn't until I became a teen and experienced intimacy with a young man that I realized this is what was done to me as a child.

I was living in fear of what would be said regarding me, when it was not me at all. For years I kept secrets and felt it was my fault. I lived to keep peace at that expense of me, the family structure is so important and the very thought of speaking about the abuse and assaults would kill my immediate family, so I thought I am more than sure it would cause a friction that we never experience out loud at least, I finally at the age of 47 exposed what happened. It seems all my life I have given and given so much of me until the hiding was now my truth. I was losing me all along. So, I would say I was fearfully and wonderfully made, but did not believe a word of it, I was not what Gods word said, well not in my eyes.

We have been taught as a culture in the black community what happens in this house stays in this house, so if the happenings were inappropriate, we kept it quiet, if the happenings were abusive, we kept it quiet. So many days I would look at myself and think only negatively about the person I saw in the mirror.

I was convinced I was not good enough, smart enough or pretty enough, or strong enough, I was ok with being in the shadow of those I looked up to along with my sisters and cousins whom I believed were the prettest girls I knew.

For decades I lived a life of inferiority, with no goal to do anything other than what someone else told me to do. All of this went on for decades, shame and embarrassment are a silent killer of ones hope and ability to overcome any obstacle we have faced in life. God did not form us to fail, however, he knew we would and provided us with his grace, mercy daily and the strength to withstand, and conquer. I heard this saying all throughout my life and still say it to this day: Tell the TRUTH and shame the devil!

CHAPTER 3 THE PRIDE OF HAIR

"But if a woman has long hair, it is her ornament and glory? for her hair is given to her for a covering."
AMP 1 Corinthians 11:15 [2]

HAIR! You may think, what does this have to do with her life story? Let me tell you it has a lot to do with it. I will remind you I grew up with sisters and my father was the one with an obsession with hair. My father met my mother when she was 16 years old, thin, very fair skinned, to be honest she looked white, but not white but mixed, and her hair was past her butt.

My dad was a persistent young man asking my mother if she wanted a ride while walking from school. She told me he would look for her every day, then one day she must have been tired of walking and telling him no, she finally said yes! And the rest is our history. They were a couple after that ride.

My father loved hair. I am not sure why, but he did. I can only remember my grandmother, his mother, wearing wigs every day of her life, when the wigs were off her hair was braided underneath a stocking cap. Could it be he grew a love for long hair from watching his mother wear wigs daily? Or did he just have a passion for long pretty hair? We will never know the answer to that question; however, the obsession did not stop with my mother it went on to his 5 daughters.

I can hear my father's voice, like it was yesterday, always giving a compliment when he sees us. "Look at that pretty hair!' As we grew older my father made sure to get us to the salon for our bi-weekly appointments, not my mother, but my dad took us and made appointments for us, wash, hot comb press and curl. Ms. Myrtle was our stylist's name, and she did not play about that hair being bone straight and curls that will last for 2 weeks.

Growing up I was blessed with a head full of hair! And it was not too bad on the texture. I had a good grade of hair. So, as you may have determined, it was a necessity in our home Saturday night that hair would be correct for Sunday morning. And you better not mess it up for school either.

Throughout the years, and growing up, we began to see the changes in hairstyles and the most popular looks. I remember as a teen I wanted a Jeri curl so bad! Everyone was wearing their hair that way, I begged until my mother finally allowed me to get my hair done that way by then I was 15 years old.

This was the beginning of a permed product in my virgin hair. I kept it up good, it was not dripping wet like the man in coming to America movie, I had great curls, it was due to the texture and grade of hair I had naturally.

After that trend was over, I went back to the straight look and added a perm to keep it straight, I had fuzzy hair that would shrink up with the humidity or rain. So, the new thing was a perm and flat irons burning my head up! Lol I can laugh about it now; however, I wish I knew then what I know

now about the tension of using these products and frying my hair with irons to keep it straight.

In this process also came the haircuts short on one side and angled exactly right on the other. Once I refuse to cut it any longer it grew back thank God, I still had a decent grade and it grew back to my shoulders, then after having children it really took off and grew past the shoulders to my rear end. I remember once I was coming home for a family event, when one of my nieces saw me, she was in shock, I was a mother of 3 at this time and was quite the plain Jane, always the natural look not a lot with make-up but just enough and modestly dressed, pretty much like the church mothers I grew up around.

They were happy to see me but stared at me the whole time, it was my hair, up in a French roll bump up top and the rest down my back. One niece could not believe it, began asking about my hair. This is why she loves that long hair to this day! She saw her auntie and had to have it. She knows who she is without me mentioning her name. You may be asking why is this chapter important or even in this book? Believe me it is all part of the journey and view of me, just keep reading.

Someone please tell me why so many men had a great obsession with a woman that had hair!

Not short hair but it had to be long, especially for the guys in church …and if you were lucky enough to have that sought after desire then you were someone to know or be with, according to the men and women who made me realize early on that the young men in church or school were always looking for that certain type. It is sad to say that my hair became my identity for many years, it was the only thing that would make me attractive, I kept it healthy and made sure it always looked good. I never imagined that one day I could lose it all.

Falling out from the root and leaving so fast it did not have time to regrow. The more I tried to care for it the more it was on the floor. I sought out several ways to get the follicles to grow back and nothing worked. Braids and weaves helped to rip the locs right out of my head I could not believe it, so the very thing that represented my identity was now gone, how do I live with that? What was I going to do? I immediately started getting hair weave styles that were like my natural hair, and I learned to care for it as if it were my own hair so much so that I thought that wearing weave or wigs no one else would know.

Well believe me they knew! It was me living in my false truth that convinced me that no one would know. One day while waiting in the church once, the pastor's daughter said to me, why do you wear wigs all the time? You never wear your real hair. It caught me off guard, but it was the awakening I needed to remove the mask, and for the first time I spoke truthfully about what I tried to hide so badly. I answered her honestly and said it would not grow in certain spots, so I had to wear them. She so innocently and very honestly said there must be something we could do to get it to grow back.

I was moved by her concern and care, she turned my attention to me and to my being honest about my current situation, and I then knew that what I thought I was hiding well, I really was not.

It was a thorn in my side, the fall out was only spots that were balding for a while, however that took a turn for the worse. And it was spreading with every worry and every style I tried.

I was living a life of secrecy because I did not feel I would be accepted the way that I was, think about it , you may have made the comments about someone yourself or heard the joke about it and laughed, the comments of being bald headed made me cringe, I hated it every time I heard someone laugh or talk about those who were without a great length of hair or with none at all made me cry on the inside. From that I knew that I would never be accepted in society, church or with any employer for that matter, if they knew and saw me for me. **I was stuck in my False Truth.**

4 WHEN LOVE GOES WRONG AT HOME

"You shall not commit adultery" AMP Exodus 20:14 [3]

The year was 1981 so many things were changing at this time, I was in high school and beginning to know a whole lot more than a young teen should of. Everyone knew my mother and father in the neighborhood, in the community and in the church. My father was a handsome black man, yes, he was.

He stood about 5'11" smooth chocolate face, great physique and always sharp, even when he came home from work! He would change his clothes out of his overalls and steel toed boots and be cleaned all up, dress shirt and dress pants hard bottom shoes; I never saw my father wear jeans or sneakers growing up, not even when he cut the grass, he would wear Stacy Adams, he would literally be working in the yard in those shoes, now who wore dress shoes to work in the yard! My Dad.

Before you ask the question how I knew what shoes they were, believe me I knew because Saturday night he sat me down with newspaper and black shoe polish a shoe brush and bung rag to shine his shoes for Sunday church service.

I remember him getting ready for church on Sundays, and every other day of the week we had to go to church, it was always a pressed suit, tie, and pocket hanky, sharp as a tac looking great and smelling good. Now I will not say that he was the only one cleaned up on those Sundays, back then men loved to dress up, clean cut, neat and suited. This was the normal attire for those I saw weekly and of course at home, my father was always presentable, and he expected no less from the rest of the family.

I remember Dad giving my sisters and I lessons outside of the house, because we had no brothers, so we learned to do what he would teach a son, cut grass, change a tire, get the tools to fix the car and he showed us how to wash the car.

Those were the tasks outside but inside; he was a great cook and took time to show us some skills inside the kitchen. What I would not give to have one of those moments again right now. Baking cakes and pies along with grilling and making sides to go along with the meals he cooked. I sure wish I had paid more attention to the recipe for his cornbread dressing! I have tried it, and it never tastes like his...these trivial things are big memories and times of family I cherish.

My handsome dad was an anointed preacher, I have only known him to be a preacher and a dedicated servant in the church that is all I knew and saw of my father's life daily. He had a voice that was calming and disposition that would capture anyone's attention without raising his voice. Now you all must know he was not all of that alone, He could not be all of that without my mother. She was not sitting in the background with everyone posing a question of why he was with her?

My sweet mother was a beautiful young woman stood about 5'0" thin was only 98 pounds at 5 months pregnant. One of the sharpest women in the church I knew, she had class, and she was not slipping on looking good as well, my father kept my mother in the best of clothes, shoes, and coats. She was modest and always well put together, I remember one time while she was getting ready for church, she would not get ready until she had all five girls together, she would get dressed last.

I remember the fancy silver comb and brush set my father gave to her, it sat on a mirrored tray with her glass bottles of perfume. One Sunday morning her using that comb and brush set, as she did most Sundays, she would flip her hair to hang in front of her, bent over with her head down, she was brushing it up to put in a pony tail, we ran into the room and she would give us the brush or comb and we would comb her hair at the bottom until she'd say "Ok that's good."

She would grab that hair flip it back, put a leather binder on it and began to braid it to the end, when it was that long past her waist near her knees, she never wore it out or down, she would pull it into a bun, she would wrap it and it filled the whole back of her head, then she would take two sticks, well I thought they were sticks and put them through the bun to hold it up. It was just beautiful; women would pay for that bun right now and they did then. My parents grew up together and raised a family and they were a notable example of a couple to me.

I often watched my mother as she was a housewife, raising her children, we always had a hot meal on the stove just in time for my dad to pull up in the driveway, and she would get the table set for him to eat, he would come in wash his hands, sit at the table, and waited for her to serve his meal in the dining room.

My sisters and I did not eat until my mother served him first. That was the rule when Dad gets home, that is when we will eat. I watched what she did and how she did it and found myself doing the same thing once I got married. She honored him as head of the household and recognized that he worked hard all day, and he was ready to come home to a peaceful clean environment. Gender roles were very prevalent in those days.

To be honest, I feel that gender roles would still work for me today, I grew up watching my mother and father take part in separate duties and caring for the home and family. I picked up those traits from them both and I am still ok with it.

Enough of that back to my journey... My father could sing you happy... my favorite is when he would stand to the mic and shake that right hand to the beat of the song and smooth lean, tapping his foot to the drum beat, and he grab the mic and began to sing an old hymn formulated by an Indian Missionary Sadhu Sundar Singh; I loved when Dad would sing my favorite part: *"Sometimes, sometimes, sometimes the road gets rough and the going gets tough and I know the hills are hard to climb, but I started out a long time ago, there is no doubt in my mind, I've decided to make Jesus my choice!"* That song was my favorite, I loved it when he sang, everyone did.

We come from an incredibly talented family, all his siblings could sing, play instruments, and or preach. That is the truth! And would do it with ease. . My siblings and I had it too, the apple didn't fall far from the tree, our whole family had talent and an anointing on our lives, I know you may be thinking I'm exaggerating with saying the whole family, but trust me I am not, every one of us carry at least one of the gifts I mentioned above. And the legacy continues with the grandchildren.

Our family, among others, had great popularity within church, and with it came relationships with many people, because of the leadership role my father had, a lot of people gravitated towards him and my mother, even if it were just to get close to my dad. All friends are not really friends, all who say they want to help does not really mean to help you, sometimes they have their own agenda to help themselves. I found that many women would be almost obsessed with my father especially at church. Well, who would not I found out that some women, will look at another woman and see what that man does for her life and began to want what that woman possesses. Truthfully, I could see why another woman would be enticed with the likes of my father, he has a great man, family oriented with a nice home, and cars, always looking well and taking care of everyone, not to add the anointing he had to preach heaven down, it was miraculous, I remember one Sunday night he was preaching, and while he was at the steps of the pulpit, all of the sudden this lady who was sitting near the front of the church, ran up to my father and was hanging all over him screaming, she was on my father like the fans you see at concerts she was hanging on him for dear life and I looked at my mother, I was sitting right next to her and she stood up and was yelling get that woman off my husband!, get that woman off of my husband!

I was scared at what was happening, I had never seen that take place in the church before. So many people ran up to that pulpit to get that lady removed from him! I can only image what my mother was feeling, she was totally outdone. They were able to get the woman off my father and he continued to preach as if nothing had happened, he was focused on the assignment at hand. I never saw other women do that again, to my father after that episode, but I did see and hear the love for him by many. It was growing with every church he preached at from all who heard him. By the time I was 15 things began to change in our home between my parents, I was the one who would catch the conversations between them, the heated conversations as well. I found out what betrayal in marriage was as a teen, and how a crushed spirit could cause you to say and do things that you normally would not do. My parents married young, not knowing what it really was except for the examples that they saw in their homes. Sometimes the sins of the father are carried down to the siblings, especially if it was never dealt with. I find that to be true about various situations and what we call generational curses.

Lifestyles, habits, addictions etc... We were in a loving family but there were things within the family that never were addressed and left the gate wide open for the generations to follow. Many families dealt with the same issues I am sure, it was handled or dealt with differently, especially if you were in the church.

My father and mother got pregnant with me out of wedlock, but married prior to me being born, hence I got pregnant out of wedlock at 16 just as my mother and father did and I remember the time I had to get up and ask the whole church to forgive me for something I had done, my getting pregnant brought shame upon the church, so I needed to be humbled and spill it in front of the same people who had whole families living in other states, the same people that would allow a young girl to be sexually assaulted by a family member, or a member of the church and treat her as if she was the issue, the same people who were abusive verbally, and sometimes physically. However, I did not understand at that time these were the people I was standing before, because hiding things was the number one correct all in the family and in the church. Hiding the truth to look perfect, holy, and sanctified was key but the family unit was dying inside the house wounded from all the secrets that had to stay in the house.

So, our house most of the time was a haven for everyone, everyone was welcomed. My mother had a passion for young people and the youth. She headed the youth department in our church, and a lot of times the young people stayed at our house. It was a gathering place most of the time. It was love, it was fun, and it was teaching as well.

My mother was nurturing and always had a listening ear. The passion came from her being a young wife and her life drastically changing when she found out she was with a child. Her life changed like day is from night. I can only imagine how she felt instantly moving in with a family she knew nothing about, instantly in the ministry and being looked up and down with a side eye because she was pregnant.

They married when she was going on 5 months and as I stated in the beginning of this book I came shortly after she got married, early! So instantly she was an adult, a mother, and a wife and had to adjust overnight. Despite the rush and sudden moves my parents had to make, they loved each other, she loved her husband, and he loved his wife. Growing up I only knew of a handful of friends my mother had. Of course, she and the other wives of the ministers and the wives of those in the singing group with my dad were closest to my mother as well as her in-laws. She had become a sister to them, and they all raised their children together. We were cousins and church cousins to the ones who were not blood related, we were all family.

Take a moment and imagine you being in this close-knit family and your circle only consisted of those you grew up around and went to church with and suddenly as quickly as you could flip a light switch or light a match here is someone that would change the whole life you knew. This is how quickly there was a change taking place in our family. All the sudden there was another woman there, I do not know where she came from, I just remember her talking to my mother and being around a lot.

This woman became close friend to our mother, she was not a minister's wife, and she was not a relative we grew up with. We will call her Mrs. Dee, Yes, she was married and a new member of the church we attended; she seemed very genuine in her presence and relationship with my mother. They talked all the time; I vividly remember one night she called our home and she stated she was afraid and had heard something outside, and there was a problem with her garage door, she wanted my father to come see what the problem was, so her good friend, my mother, listened and was frightened for her and asked my father to go see about her, because her husband wasn't home, so there he went and our whole lives changed after that night.

He went and was gone a good while, he did back sometime that night after I guess everything was secured at her home, however, I'm going to give my opinion on what I believed, I don't really believe anything was going on at her home, I believe she wanted an opportunity to be alone with the man she really wanted. 📌 I will stick a pin in here to remind you that my father has been with my mother since they were teens, and she was only with him, that we know of, they were teenagers and fell in love, had a baby.

I remember the older in the family women use to say, talking grown folks talk, never have your husband go to another women's house alone or never trust a woman who summons your husband, it was always said watch the ones who stay in a husband face, without the wife there, giving the connotation that women could not be trusted with someone else's man because they were often after them. That stuck in my head all these years. Believe me I learned this first-hand as well. I am sure that there are many who are reading this, and your mouth has fallen wide open, and you cannot believe it...

well believe it. My father had an extramarital affair, and it broke our home up. The most devastating thing to happen in our lives. I watched them change and it wasn't so pretty, I cannot speak on what my father may have been thinking at that time, and why he would give in to the temptation of this women, or if this was the only time, or had it been multiple times, I don't know and will never know, He had a beautiful wife and a lovely family at home.

Now this is a grown-up Cherelle talking right here in this book, it is not the 15-year-old that witnessed trauma without understanding of what happened. My parents had an active sex life, hence all of us being born and the reason our room would be taken over at times, it took me a while, but I figured it out. Our bedroom had a big lock on the door, we could never use the lock but when he came home, they used the lock! You can imagine my mother's face when I, as an adult, told her I knew what was going on in that room! We busted out in laughter, she could not believe I was saying this to her; however, I was not making it up.

Back to this journey, my mother found out after that visit to her best friends, they are relationship was not much of a relationship anymore, they rarely spoke to each other anymore, the best friend began to distance herself from my mother, and it began to be a struggle with conversations.

This woman was nothing like my mother, she did not look like her, she was brown skinned, short, and fuller figured and had a short haircut... I will say right here there is nothing wrong with full figured women, hence I am now a full-figured woman, and there is nothing wrong with brown-skin or short hair, this is my 14/15 -year-old self-thinking what and why?

My belief is that no matter the exterior package of anyone, something on the interior was able to capture the attention of my father, so much so that he chose to do what he probable never planned to do … and start a roller coaster ride to the demise of his family. My question all these years is, what would cause a man who has everything he wanted, or we thought, make a decision that could tear down all that he built with a wife, family, and home. Eventually my father told my mother what had been done and explained that he was sorry, yes, I said he told her, I know he could have gotten away with it, but he told her and then apologized, believing all would be okay, but it did not mend my mother's broken heart or the lack of trust and betrayal she felt, that was clearly going to take some healing. And let alone the fact that it was her best friend or so-called friend, the knowledge of her friend and her husband being intimate was a hard one to just let go. I know you are asking; how do I know all of this? Well I was the one who had to hear my mother crying, and all the arguing about this situation and the betrayal that happened. Believe me, prior to writing this I spoke with my mother just to get her approval and she was shocked! She never knew that I had heard everything that was going on, it was a sad situation; she was treated poorly from family and the church, because they did not really know what or why this was happening, she never discloses to everyone what had happened for the sake of my dad and him being in ministry. Through the hurt and pain, she chose to cover him. She held it and it crushed her.

Our family dynamic changed, it was not long either, they divorced because of this, everyone looked at my mother as the evil one and I hated it. I hated that this had happened to her, I hated that my siblings and I were now outcasts. Because of the divorce.

I do not know if my father ever thought that he could save this family and keep us together, all I know when the divorce was over, he was even more of a church celebrity than before. And most times we were forgotten, not by everyone but by a lot of people and family, everyone was loyal to my father, it was because everyone loved him so much.

We had no real explanation for what was going on, but my sisters and I knew it was not good, after the divorce my father moved to the back of the house until he would get a place to stay... and when he did, he moved all the way to the west side of town. Now he would come and check on us from time to time or he would surprise us when we would come home after school, he would be sitting on the porch steps. He was trying to keep a presence there. Who wouldn't? He had five girls, five daughters and was no longer in the home... the decision that they made impacted us heavily, you see the mistakes my sisters and I made were often blamed on my mother because my father was not in the home, I didn't think that was fair judgment, our mother did the best she could with us girls.

After dealing with the reality of all this, there was a great feeling of rejection that came upon me, after a while we slowly but surely faded out of the picture and out of his daily life as priority and we were forgotten.

Now I am certain that the decision my father made after the divorce was not a happy one. Him no longer in our home we had to learn to do things on our own, my mother had to get a job, she had never worked before.

Visitations were scheduled for my dad to get us, and we would sit for hours waiting and most times he did not come. I experienced what divorce did to the family and swore that I would never in my life get a divorce. Remember I said earlier what is not dealt with in one generation will magnify in the next, remember that. I am definitely certain that my dad never thought that his daughters would deal with all the life challenges we faced, sexual assaulted, abuse, poverty, insecurity, and no knowledge of how to date or even choose the right guy, we were so longing for attention and love from the absence of our father that when presented by a guy we thought this was great and the real thing. To have someone who claimed they loved us, unfortunately, we ended up with men who took advantage of us, abused us, and used us to the point of brainwashed and settling for the abuse be it physical, mental, and emotional.

We were not prepared for any of this at all; however, and despite the distance that became our new normal with our dad, we his daughters love our father regardless of what the relationship was or grew to be. I tried as long as I could to stay close and be connected to him.

When I was able to drive and get to his church I would, most times when I spoke of who my dad was, various women would try to use that to get close to me for my dad, he was a fine Pastor and single, but that did not work at all. He eventually did remarry and as I stated in the introduction, he had more children. 🎣 I will stick a pin in right here. Now everyone deserves happiness and someone to share their life with, no one just wants to grow old alone, I remember my friends told me about my father being engaged, yes, I said my friends from church. I did not believe it at all, they told me all about his wife to be and I sat in shock, I was living in Columbus, Ohio at the time.

I remember finally calling my dad to ask about what everyone was telling me, I wanted to see if it was true and surely it was, now, I was happy and shocked when I asked about his fiancé, and when we were going to meet her, he responded, for what? I just thought since she would be part of the family, she would want to meet his 5 children... and I slipped up and said to my father "well what about us?" and he replied to me "What about you?" At that point I left it alone, those words I have never forgotten, nor did I forget, what I felt as a teenager, it all came back to the forefront of my mind at the age of 25, we were going to be outcasts again, and forgotten. It just felt like we were pushed aside.

We were invited to the wedding, surprisingly. However, my dad wanted his siblings there and had me to be the driver for all the family, he rented a van and I had to pick everyone up and take them to the wedding. I cannot say that we felt like she would take us all in. At this time in life, we began to see a lot of blended families.

I am a witness to the blended family because I ended up with a blended family of 8 and I never treated them as outsiders or treated them as a burden to our relationship, what we did for one we did for all, when you saw one of us you saw all of us. We were a family who never pinned anything against each other, and we raised them all well with love, compassion, care, and security. To this day all my children are still as close as they were when they were kids, and they had the opportunity to experience what a blended family is and should be, we were truly one family.

When my father passed away in 2019, he left a legacy behind, he had 8 children, 16 grandchildren and 23 great grandchildren, some of the eldest grands he had the opportunity to know and have a relationship with. Many may not have known this, however there were a lot of people from the time of my mother and father that knew we existed and acknowledged us.

What got me the most at my father's home-going services and was so sad, when we had to process in at his services and everyone looking at us trying to figure who we were, all I could hear is "oh that must be the daughters," or "oh they must be the girls." We looked good, and we were brought up with class and we were there to honor our father... so, I now know in my own life that ministry, distance, and even family can keep you from having time to spend with the ones you love.

Remember this is my journey and my view, I will never forget the family bible studies we had, my father would cut everything off and it was bible lesson time and family prayer. I am grateful for the times I would see my father kneeling in the dining room always on the left chair on one knee praying and praying, our weekly practices in the back room because my sisters and I had to sing on the broadcast and my father was making sure we would be ready and that we practiced!

I will never forget those moments...some people inherit finances and tangible things, and if you were or are fortunate enough to receive those things that is great! My sisters and I, what we received is more than anything money could buy, it is having our memory of good times with our father. This is what we pass down to our children, they will always know who their grandfather and great grandfather was. This is our inheritance.

Now for those who are reading this and saying why would she do this and why would she say that about her father and family? I will tell you why...because what has been hidden for many years did nothing but magnify in the children affected by it. I refuse to allow what I endured to magnify or continue in my children or my grandchildren, my nieces, and nephews. It must stop somewhere so there is no better place than with me, and it is my life's journey, and I am not going to paint it so people will be comfortable with it, what I felt and have lived with for years is a real thing, what I have endured was a real thing and I am finally bold enough to say what and how things affected me and how they impact my life. With all that I saw and heard within my parents' relationship, and the relationship with the church and members, left me dealing with a lot of issues, mentally, and emotionally. A lot of people looked at us from the outside, we were beautiful young ladies, but never took the time to see what damage we had on the inside due to the love being lost in our home, five daughters without their father over physical pleasure. I won't put all the blame on him, he could of been grossly seduced by this woman friend and didn't know how to react, I'll just say, young man or old man if you don't know what to do, think about what your family might end up being without you, then run away from her fast, she will not be worth it. The weight of brokenness, rejection, and hollow love. It is a hurtful or empty space that no one can fill. I tell you who helped us through it all and that was and is Jesus Christ and the love of God. The Holy Spirit comforts and keeps us when we did not think we would make it after being broken, battered, and bruised, but God says I still have use of you. I love you and I feel your pain. That pain and discomfort has taught us to be strong and to love God and to care about family more than ever.

If ever you have a question concerning children who may be the product of a divorce, know that the discomfort and loss goes beyond the parents. Truth and not hiding would have helped us as we moved into adulthood. The pain of not being acknowledged is a pain that will never be forgotten but it is forgiven even if they never asked us to forgive them. That is how you move on in your truth. Admit it, acknowledge it, and move on from it.

I Thank God for my foundation in him and the undying love he has for his children. Without Christ I cannot imagine how the situations and circumstances in my life and my sisters' lives would have turned out. Now let me put this last disclaimer here, I know my father loved my sister and I. I know he cared for us, and I pray he thought of us often. What was done was done, we were still his children no matter how old we would get we still wanted that father's approval, that security in knowing it would be ok because dad said it would be ok, and no, we were not some bastards by a hap hazard woman our parents were kids themselves having kids and just like some of us, they grew up while raising their children, there is no perfect way to do it, it is just knowing you tried to be the best at it is all that matters. Always a daddy's girl.

CHAPTER 5 IT LOOKED LIKE LOVE, BUT IT WAS ONLY LUST...

"For all that is in the world, the lust of the flesh, and the lust of the eyes, and the pride of life, is not of the Father, but is of the world." AMP 1 John 2:16 [4]

This chapter pulled me back to the place of living false truths and hiding to make the men in my life look good and without flaw. I was sexually assaulted as a child that ended when I was about 11 years old, the crazy part is I blocked those years out. I forgot until a flash from my past came flooding in like a river that is flowing with heavy rapids. I mentioned in the introduction, I was in high school when the memories of my young body laying across a bed being poked and rubbed, kissed and groped by someone who should of never touched me in that way in the first place, I remember his nasty stinking breath and clammy lips and tongue and stinking body makes me want to vomit right now. I only realized it after I had my boyfriend in the 11th grade, who did those same things to me, it made me realize that I should not have had any encounter with a relative of mine at all.

I suppressed the thought of it as a child, being told you better not tell anybody! And you are scared to tell someone for fear of repercussions from the one who assaulted you. That is how I began this life of covering up and holding on to the issues that would later take its toll on me.

I became a mother incredibly young, that boyfriend in high

school was never a life partner for me, honestly, I tell you I didn't know what the heck I was doing with this boy but the result of one time, because you know all it takes is one time and here comes a child. Hell, he even denied my son was his until he saw him after he was born, and he came out looking just like him and his family.

I was on my own with my oldest child, I took care of him, and I was responsible for him financially.

I was a teen mom, and I did feel ashamed about it, but I never let it stop me from being a mother to my son, Anthony, he grew up with me, I was only 16 when I brought him into this world. I worked and went to school and the following school year I graduated with a 1-year-old son.

I would not change it for nothing, he has grown up into a fine young man and he takes care of his family. It was not easy at all, but we made it through. As he says, Mom we have been rolling together for 40 years! Yes, we have, and I have never been prouder of him than I am with each new day. So back to this journey, high school is over. I have been on my own for some years now and I have had a few children by the age of 25. Between 16 and 25 I have had 2 serious boyfriends and here I am young adult 28 years old, never married, the relationship I thought would be forever with my 2nd son's father was not my forever and I am thinking, my sisters are already married, and I still do not have a husband.

My cousins were married and here is me? I have had 2 babies and no husband; truth be told I did not only have 2 babies at this time but 2 abortions, yes, covering up for church guys, in my life I have had 2 real relationships, after my oldest son's father.

And each one was with a young man brought up in church, I remember my boyfriend at the time we were about 18 years old, we had been friends for a long time due to our parents and church relationship, when we got old enough to really date, we did for a few years, and within those years we were sexually active, and we got pregnant.

He wasn't happy about it at all, he was worried about the church and his reputation...so he decided what we would do about the pregnancy, and he made an appointment for me, picked me up one day and took me to this place I didn't know of to have an abortion, because he wasn't ready to have a child, definitely not out of wedlock, I remember it like yesterday, we arrive there and on this cold table I lay, tears running down my face uncontrollably, I could hardly breath, I was scared to death, and I really didn't want to do this, I hear the doctor come in and he examined me, and when he pulled his hand out from under the sheet, his glove was full of blood and he says she is losing this baby!

I was in the middle of a miscarriage, from all the stress of being told I had to do this, I was so scared I could not tell anyone what was going on. The doctor turns on a loud machine and I feel my insides being sucked out of me, the doctor finishes the procedure, and I am no good, I was in pain and emotionally distraught, he looked at me saying I will be all right. I cried all the way home. I cried for many days; I was dealing this invasion in my body and now the fear of just going to hell because of what I have done, my mind was all over the place, that was the longest ride home ever, you know the most insensitive and hurtful part of that ride home. He decides to visit his friend in college!

I am in the car bleeding life out of me, and he goes to hang out with his friend. I was over it with him for that, I really was distraught for years, and the crazy part about it every year he would make me relive that time always calling and reminding me of the day and reminding me of the month and how old the child would be, it drove me crazy!I would subject myself to that anguish repeatedly, going with It thinking he must have felt bad about the issue or wanted me to think that he did. If he wanted to be that attached to the child, why put me through all of that? Why did he take me to get rid of the child? it left me for and emotional and mentally unstable mess for year.

I would pray to God for forgiveness for doing something like this, the guilt of what I had done to help cover up this act of sexual activity outside of marriage. I was sliding down a very slippery slope of emotional depression, and guilt, after that I told no one! Here I go again holding on to secrets that were killing me on the inside, as I smiled on the outside. I told no one of the sexual assault that I endured and now I cannot tell anyone of the traumatic experience that took place in my body and mind so he would not look bad.

The second one came years later I was in my twenties this was my next real relationship that never ended up as I thought it would, I dated this man for over 8 years and he had no real plans to marry me, I was devastated, pretty much felt like a fool after all this time, I end up with another child, I birthed one and we dispersed of this next one, I told him about the 2nd child, and I remember clearly the statement he uttered "what is everybody in the church going to say, I'm just out here having babies" I then felt he didn't want the child and I had to keep a good image for church so here is another place that I take the road of covering up again. I honestly thought that if I did what he wanted he would want me even more, I thought I would be the one he would marry.

I began to think that I was not good enough to build this family with, that relationship was over after this, I suffered the anguish of a child being ripped from my insides to make him happy, not knowing I would suffer this forever feeling of loss, embarrassment, and shame. I felt less than for putting myself through that and kept quiet about it all these years. I began to feel the weight of rejection and never good enough for anyone.

I gave myself to these two men, who said they loved me and wanted me they and loved God, and I tried being who I thought they were looking for in a young woman but still and yet I was not enough, or good enough, seems I was just good to play with, have a good time with but not enough for them to want life with.

I could not believe I had waited all these years and still had no real commitment. I felt like a fool and as I am writing this, I am emotional all over again. You see when you really love someone you love them, no matter the hurt that may have been caused it does not remove the fact that you had genuine feelings for them, and you loved them honestly.

Now it took some time but, He did realize some years later that it was all wrong, and he expressed how sorry he was for putting me through all of that with the abortion, with the other women, and wasting my time. I wonder often what if I had stood up for myself?

Would it have gone this way? Would we be together now? Could I have saved myself from the trauma of covering the turmoil of going through the detachment of my child again! What if I had just kept the child and raised it alone? I will never know, however, the weight of guilt that I carried was killing me, I was so ashamed of myself and felt I did not even deserve to have any more children, but I did, God still blessed me even after I had done the unthinkable.

I cried out and prayed so much asking God to forgive me for what I had done, I asked him to please forgive me, I said it over and over again. My heart was hurting so bad, the weight of suffering in silence and living like all was well was killing me, not knowing that the stress I was carrying on the inside would eventually show up on the outside. I would pray and pray and one day while on the floor praying again God answered me, replied I have forgiven you! You must forgive yourself!

That part right there shook my whole being. I was continuing to throw shame on myself and never forgave ME! I then began learning to forgive Cherelle... it was a journey, because I was still ashamed and afraid to tell anyone what I had to hide. The opinion of others mattered way too much in my life, that is why I ended up the way I did. I just allowed what people expected of a Pastors daughter to shape my life and it was a big fat lie! I was not as good as everyone thought. I had harbored some real resentment in my heart, and I hated what I had become. I felt like nothing.

If you look there was a pattern here. I longed for acceptance and love so I figured the way to have them love me was to give myself to them and they would love me back. I was living a life hiding my truth, I was never supposed to give myself away to these men, and I paid for it physically and mentally because of it.

Now, I am sure there are questions on why I would not do something about it so I would not end up pregnant, I did do something, and I still got pregnant, so birth control did not work for me. Now, I have had 2 real boyfriends and ended up with 2 husbands seems like a whole lot.

Spending years with each of these men not 1 year or 2 years but 9,10 plus years that yield the result in me to this day still being alone. I will not say I wasted my time, but I will say to you reading this, your time is valuable, choose wisely, I pray no one will have to go through years of rejection, accepting false dreams, honestly, I never thought I would have anyone else due to me being a single mother back then, not many men especially in church would want someone with a child. I was looking for love, looking for companionship, looking for acceptance, and a fairytale happily ever after and it still has not happened yet and that is my Truth!

6 WHEN LOVE GOES WRONG FOR ME

"Let marriage be held in honor (esteemed worthy, precious, of great price, and especially dear) in all things."
AMP Hebrews 13:4 AMP [5]

Now, this time it is a whole different type of relationship, I will be honest and tell my truth on this here, this relationship was on the rebound of the one with my 2nd son's father. I wanted to get away from him so badly when I got the attention of someone else, I took it and ran with it, I was not looking for It, but it happened and here I go again this is another in the church. This time he is licensed to preach.

Only to know that everything that looks wholesome is not. This is unreal after all the hurt of relationship I am still wishing for a lifelong partner, love, and security; you ever hear the term you got to do what you have never done to get what you have never had? Well, my employer offered me a promotion and it required me to relocate and to open a few offices south of Ohio. I moved to get settled, myself and my 2 boys adjusting from having a lot of family support to having no one in the city that we knew personally, was hard. I tried finding a local church to attend as well.

I found one I was invited to visit by a young lady who came to my new office, I went and decided to visit there. It was a small family church a little different than what I was used to, but I thought why not try it. There was a young man on the drums, he was making his way over to speak to me and finding out who I was.

Everyone was happy about me being there, could be because I mentioned who my father was and where I came from, they knew who he was and were glad I was in the church. As time went on, the young man kept pursuing me and I was alone in a city did not know anyone and took the chance on the young Preacher, surely, he would be ok to talk to. Honestly now he caught me at a vulnerable state in my life. I had broken up with my long-term boyfriend and not long ago go through the horrific procedure of an abortion and was truly vulnerable.

I moved forward with this young man without knowing his story, what he did or what he was into just thinking he was saved and a preacher this should be ok. It was not, we proceeded to date and hang out with his family, and 6 months later he asked to marry me, I said yes, and the roller coaster began. I had been on my own since the age of 17 years old, taking care of bills, groceries, rent, and car note all alone. He had never had any of those responsibilities and it showed, however we moved forward with the relationship and finally I got to have a wedding and a husband. After the wedding he moved into the place I had because he did not have a place, he was still living at home with parents.

This is hilarious, I remember after the wedding was over he took the money box and made sure to count it out, now mind you it was most of my friends and family who gave us anything, but he took everything! He rolled the money up in his pocket and I think if I remember correct, I got a t-shirt from the mall and we spent one night at a hotel, then to his family's home to sleep on the floor that was my honeymoon.

It was nothing I expected, only to sleep on the floor at his siblings house.

He never put any thought into anything for us, just what he would gain, he was finally out of his parents' home and took all the money for himself. That should have been a red flag for me right there.

As I used to do prior to marriage, I went out of town to see my youngest child at the time my second son who was living with his father due to my work situation we will touch on that a little later in the journey. I returned home and my new husband was there with his friends. I walked in to see a big screen tv, and noticed he purchased another sports car. Nothing was discussed and no financials reviewed, red flag, irresponsibility issue with spending. I did go ahead to ask about the purchases, the discussion was not heated but I was very disturbed by it. I come home to an apartment, my apartment full of his friends and this TV. Then it was a guitar, then another car! Clothes and shoes, I could not understand why his money was his and he could do whatever he wanted with it. Even if it meant utilities being cut off. Next red flag was him going out of town for few days on the weekends, no calls no show, no explanation nothing, I was devastated, angry and felt so stupid for falling for this young man who had nothing to offer me, but heartache.

Early in the marriage I began to see something different for me, he would leave to stay out of town with an ex-girlfriend, who was pregnant with his child. Another thing that everyone in his family tried to hide and convince me that he was over her. I put up with a lot of extra drama, disrespect, and abuse in this marriage.

The blatant disrespect towards me and for me because he really wanted to be with the other girl, I feel we could have avoided this whole fiasco and he could have been with his forever sweetheart, why drag me into this crazy mess, that is what I meant by everything that looks wholesome may not be that at all. I now was experiencing this abuse I had never had. There was nothing I could ever say to him, it was always stupid, I knew nothing about what he was doing, I was suddenly in a warp speed of losing myself. He would be angry if I did not watch porn with him, I had never even seen that kind of stuff, but he was dead on it. Opening a whole other spiritual war between us.

I did not care for it, and he knew it but somehow, he always projected back to me being nothing, and needed to learn some things to please him as he saw on the pornography he was addicted to watching.

I began losing confidence in myself and I had no self-esteem, nothing hurts worse than the person you chose to love not loving you back. I stayed in this loveless marriage for about 10 years to be exact, however, I could not take it anymore, the verbal abuse, infidelity, the lack of being taken care of and financially in ruins.

He had a way of making me feel less than a person, embarrassed not just at home either, it got so bad he would do it anywhere church on Sunday, at the grand old church conventions, wherever it did not matter he could not cover it up if he wanted to, his face always showed it. I remember once in Cleveland, he left me stranded at the convention, left without me, and did not come home.

He stayed overnight there in Cleveland, because he did not want me there in the first place. I had to get a ride home from the convention that was ridiculous! Thank God for a sister friend and her husband who saw it all and offered me a ride back home. I often expressed how bad I felt to the women at the church the leaders who advised I could not discuss anything about our marriage to anyone who was not a minister's wife, so I said nothing except to them and the advice returned often was just don't say anything, don't ask him questions just pray about it, it was always just pray about it. And I did pray because I wanted this to be right. I knew what divorce did for me and my siblings so I swore I would not get a divorce; I would stay to work it out for better or worse.

Lord knows I was trying to be right and do all I could to make this work. At this point what I held in emotionally began to come out physically. I started losing weight quickly. I was thin without trying, and the hair I had down my back began to fall out daily. My hair would just come out at the touch in handfuls. Prior to him I had beautiful hair and every day I watched it get thinner and thinner and spots began to show through, I was so stressed out but so busy trying to look like everything was ok when it was not. I had never had a problem with my hair falling out, but this was the beginning of my demise. I never spoke to my family about what was going on in my marriage, and I did not get to see them often either during this time I even lost years with my son who was with his father, I will speak more on that later in the journey.

I remember a time when I it got so bad, I was plotting to hurt this husband of mine, that's how you know I no longer needed to be there,he was gone for 4 days and I had the house dark and was just waiting for him come home and come through the door, at this time I had 4 children I had two girls with him, they were home with me all the time so we are in this house its dark and I was waiting for him to come home, but before he did somehow his parents called ask for him and I tell them he is not here. I do not know if it was the way I said it or my tone, but they miraculously got to my home quickly, he finally pulled up at home and began to come through the door, there I stand with the largest knife I had and ready to slice him up!

I was so angry and devastated by this repeated act of disrespect that I wanted him to feel the same hurt that I had. His parents got there as I stated and somehow came through the back door and grabbed my hand in the air before I hurt him. It was a scene that could have been in a movie, I was ready to end it all. I was mentally distraught, and I began to hate him, I know hate is a strong word, but I just could not take it anymore.

I know it was God saving me by sending his parents there, I would have lost my children for doing something like this, it was horrible. I looked like a mentally unstable person; my demeanor and countenance were not me at all. I had become someone I did not even know existed in me, I was just fed up with the fake happy marriage view that I had to put on every week for the people at church, my home was not a home, I was living in pure hell. This was my distorted view in living color, everyone looked at me I was clean, and I was dressed as well as I could be, after being stripped of the clothing I had prior to marrying him, I was not allowed to wear the clothes I had because he was a minister, then turned Elder. So, I was homely and depressed just image that look!

I was afraid to say how I felt for it meant nothing to him. I watched how divorce tore my family up as a child and I swore I would marry for life, and everything that was happening showed me this was going to be a horrible life. I just could not take it anymore, I felt like I was stuck in a nightmare.

After his parents saved me from trying to take him out that day, they left and took him with them, the same day the landlord came to our home and it was because the rent was past due, she knocked on the door and I hesitated to answer but she didn't leave, so I open the door and she looks at me with a surprised facial expression, and asked can she come in, I let her in, and the house was in total darkness I had every window closed and no sunlight coming in anywhere, the kids sitting in the middle of the floor and I looked like death.

She began to ask me questions with a look of worry on her face, and I would answer her vaguely, she asked if I was alright and I told her yes, she asked me again with a greater concern in her voice, and I looked up at her and said no with tears in my eyes, she grabs me hugs me and tells me I will be alright, now at this point she sees me after this huge altercation with him finally coming home and I was in a horrible mindset, a very dark place in my life.

I never knew what this feeling of worthlessness, anger and hatred was, and why this had to be my life, surprisingly this Caucasian woman in my living room began to talk to me and tell me about the love of Jesus Christ, now you all know, that I knew about the love of Jesus Christ but this weight of depression had a hold on me I couldn't do anything all day but cry... this woman began to pray for me and speak life over me and my children, she went throughout the house and opened every window every curtain and began to let light in the rooms.

She went to her car, and she brought me this case of video tapes to watch, they were a woman's conference videos and so, I accepted them from her, and promised I would watch them. After that exchange she gave me extra time to get the rent turned in. After she left, I just sat on the couch in tears, praying to God to help me, to take me out of this rut I was in.

I was so ashamed and so hurt that I no longer wanted to be there. Mind you, I never spoke to my family about this, I lived in a city away from all my family and felt I had no support. I was too ashamed to tell anyone my marriage was a joke, and I was living in depression. I began to listen to the tapes, and they helped me to have some hope that things would not always be like this, and God would help me. Me and my children would be okay. When I finally chose to leave southern Ohio and come home, I came with 10.00 in my pocket and half a tank of gas, I packed my children's clothes and left everything else behind. I had nothing but it was everything to gain some peace. I looked so bad, the stress of this relationship was more than I could take, and yes there were other issues with infidelity and court ordered community service that had to take place because of choices he made, that was it for me I had no trust in this marriage, I knew he didn't care for me; I spoke to my father of course after the fact and he gives me away to this person, he told me when he saw me, "You don't have to live beneath your standards and means for anyone" also "You should never be with or marry someone who has less than you."

I listened and because of my experience and the pain of divorce I tried to stick it out, however it became the best thing for me and my children. I am grateful that God supplied and kept his hands on me and my family, it was not easy, but he kept us, provided for us, and gave me the security of family when I returned to my home. **I finally had to tell them my Truth, I finally saw myself for who I really was, I looked in the mirror and cried I was broken down and hated what I seen, what I saw was me.**

CHAPTER 7
WHEN LOVE GOES WRONG FOR ME AGAIN

"Husbands love your wives, as Christ love the church and gave Himself up for her." AMP Ephesians 5:25 [6]

Let us move ahead some, Finally, I am divorced from husband number 1 and working on me, I am back at home surrounded by my family. Now is the time for me to focus on building my family back up again. This task took a few years to do, just getting established with basic needs was an accomplishment.

I was living with my baby sister for a little while, but she had her own family there and our mother, so I knew it would not be for long, I just slept on the floor and the kids were with their cousin in their room. It was tight but she would never have me out on the street with two children. I finally got a chance to move into an old home that was not in the best condition, but I could afford it, I was not charged rent to stay there I just needed to cover the utilities.

So, I took the old, rugged space painted and cleaned it up as well as I could, so that we could have a place to live. It worked for a little while, about 10 months, until the roof fell in on us after a storm in the area and I needed to move.

I was grateful for a place to stay and with it being someone like family I wonder why they did not make sure it was structurally safe for me and my children, this could have been a deadly accident. This was horrific and I was not in a place to pay any expensive rent, not having any support from the kids' father yet and me working part-time meant low-income housing. Due to the issues with the roof falling in I was able to get into a place with government assistance, they helped get me into an apartment and it was a total blessing. We had a home now, and I felt safe there. Things were looking up for us.

I had a part-time job, and I went back to school part time and had a new place to live. Being home was good. I remember a day when I was working at this check cashing office and a man walks in that I know and knew him very well.

He comes in like he wants information on the loans offered. He was not looking for a loan at all, he was looking for me. Yes, looking for me, he heard I was back in town and set his goal out to find me, and he did. We were friends when I was a teen, now all grown up he comes back to see if we could restore the friendship. I am cordial glad to see him we talked briefly about our families then we exchanged numbers, and he leaves.

So, after he left called me and continued to call until we set a date up, we went to dinner, nothing fancy it was a local breakfast spot, we ate laugh and talked for hours. I was not in the place of trying to have a relationship so of course I was hesitant, but he is persistent and continues to pursue me. I have been through this past relationship, and I have children, girls at that to think about. I did eventually give in to his persistence and we built a great friendship turned into a relationship, well I thought it was great, this was slow and steady, and he was always respectful.

I must say he was this was totally the opposite of what I had previously experienced, working, taking care of his family, and knowing what he wants in life. I was certain that he would be better than any man that I was with he genuinely cared for me and my children and especially the one who was not with us in New York. This man was systematically and intentional in disarming and removing every fear I had about being in a relationship with a man again.

When there was a need, he just did it. I did not ask for it, he just handled it. Made sure I had what I needed without requesting or wanting anything in return, this went on for 3 years before I married him, he was and still is a great man provider and father. He was a key factor in bringing all my family back together and I am forever grateful for his help and support in rebuilding my family. Throughout this time the stress level is lower than before, and I am working on getting out of a depressed state. Home, church and now a good old friend was all working in my favor. I began to let the walls down and allow someone to help me, to love me and be a significant help in my life. I remember it clearly, me at home on valentine's day evening, he had to work midnights that night, so I knew we were not going to dinner or anything. He gets off early in the morning and comes to my apartment, to give me box of chocolates and a red rose, I was excited and thanked him then as I sat on my couch, he gets down on one knee and asks me to marry him! I am shocked because we spoke about marriage in the beginning and he promised he would never get married again, and I was okay with it especially after my marriage. I sat in shock and with tears in his eyes he asked me again, I replied yes!

We hugged and kissed and off he went, he had to go to his day job. This was a wonderful time in our lives, we planned what we wanted for the wedding and set a budget for it all. It was the most stress-free, worry-free wedding I had ever seen. It was beautiful and we had the support of both our families and our children. Many years passed, and we have raised all the children, except my last when she was still in high school. Things began to look low in this relationship as there were too many nights I spent alone and vacations that I could not be a part of. I was heavy in ministry, and he was heavy in his fraternity.

I began to get calls at home from women, I would get messages from his friends' wives that you never go anywhere, meaning that I did not go with my husband to parties or outings in clubs and what have you, I was not social enough. And I will admit I didn't go to clubs and I didn't hang out, the only time he would try to ask me to go somewhere it would be a pajama party with the fraternity and I would not subject myself to that I was an Elder in my church and I didn't know how that would look for me in ministry.

Now let me tell you, I believe when you have a breakup each person plays a part in it. You must own your part. I was reluctant to have a social background when he met me, and he knew I was not the type to frequent clubs' dances or bars. But now that I was married to him, he expected those things even if it went against my moral standards. Well, I did not do it, and some may say that is why he cheated. I do not know if that is correct, but as for my part I should have spoken up about the way it made me feel when he did not come home or when he went away on vacation without me.

I fail to believe that is why he would have extramarital relations outside of our marriage. It was a choice he made, he never stops seeing other women throughout our time of engagement and brought it right into our marriage, I just did not know about it. I was a great wife, not a perfect wife, but he had no complaints about me being loving, accepting, and willing to raise all our children. I love being married, and I took great care of our family. No one deserves to be mistreated and dishonored at all. I remember twice when I realized we were really in two different worlds. My husband rarely came to church with me, many did not even know I was married and if they did know they did not know who. I remember a time in church one of the young ladies I was acquainted with saw him come in church he was seated, and she said to someone else oh no, she said, that is and she called my husband's name and the person she was talking to said yes that is Cherelle's husband.

And she replied he is not married that is, and she named another woman's name, boyfriend they been together for years. Wow, as my mother stood there and heard the whole conversation it was quite embarrassing. I did not know what to say to that comment, of course he denied it and tried to laugh it off. Whenever he was lying, he did that sly laugh as to say oh crap she knows! Another time after this had happen, I was at a social dinner and some of his co-workers for the city and county were there, and one lady I knew we will call her Ms. S. and I proceeded to speak to her in passing and she then decides to introduce me to the other ladies at the table and introduces me as my husband's wife, they look and say who? She says his name again and one of her girlfriends proceeds to say, oh so and so's man, I stand there in disbelief and replied, what did you say? And she says to me "oh it's okay girl, I would choose you over her anyway!" Nice to meet you! with this weird smile on her face, I will admit currently I was fuming! I could not believe these women would say all of this to my face. I have names but I will not disclose them but to this day I still do not care for any of them. No one hurts another woman like another black woman. They knew exactly what they were doing, and it was just another time of exposure to who I was really married to.

Of course, I went back to him and told everything word for word, and he was in shock. That was the beginning of all hell breaking loose in our marriage for years I was disrespected, and I felt like a failure again. One of his girlfriends has got bold and began to come to my place of worship and tell people that I was her man's wife! sitting right up front and trying to get a reaction from me, I never gave into it. I had self-respect and there were people along with my children watching me.

So, I did and said nothing every week. What I found out is, you cannot make someone be faithful to you if they do not want to be. Unlike my first marriage I cannot say he did not care for me or love me because I know that he did.

It was something more, when you break trust, it is hard to get it back. Especially when the person is in denial about their actions that caused the lack of trust. I currently am more mature and wiser in handling my responsibilities. This transition and divorce was devastating and full of tension, we both were hurting and fighting, neither of us was functioning at our best and we did not know how to fix it we tried counseling and that was a flop it did not work for us and I tried on my own to fix it with surprise trips for us, trying to get away from the chaos that we had invited into our lives, but that didn't work either. The way he saw it being fixed was for me to get over it! Literally the words he said several times, I just couldn't get over the fact that you would drag me through your dysfunction and disrespect, when all I did was respect you and the vows we made. We parted as loyal friends with heavy hearts, I did not want to hate him or become a bitter woman, so I chose to treat my husband with continued respect and care. Many asked me over and over why are you being so nice to him? Why do you care about him? my answer was I want to have love again in my life, so I will not treat him with disrespect and hatred that will hinder or stop me from experiencing what love God has for me in the future. Be careful how you treat those who treat you wrong. The bible tells us to love them not to hate them and I portrayed that throughout the whole divorce process and did it sincerely. God has never lied or refused me a promise that he has made to me. And I am grateful for this man that my children call Dad. He has never failed them as a father or as a provider, for that I am grateful. We are the best of friends and have the most respect for each other.

Unlike my previous marriage I did not have a sense of what I am going to do now? This time I felt completely free and a weight of relief over my life, God was with me and kept me sane throughout this transition. Real love will not go away. It stays. I am not speaking of physically going away, but true love does just that it loves and sometimes the type of love given or even felt needs a new definition and direction.

Growth and maturity will allow you to see that. The mirror of distortion was here as well, we looked good we lived good but at the end of it, his words to me about the infidelity were, just get over it, and stay in the marriage, however, I could not. I have finally come to a place of respecting Cherelle when others did not. I know my worth now and I know what I will accept and not accept in a relationship, I was not in the business of openly sharing my husband with whomever, I was not putting myself at risk anymore.

So, the divorce happened, many were shocked to even hear of the divorce, because I never put his business in the street, I did not speak on what was done to me I was still covering him and his reputation. He was messing it up enough on his own with the many ladies that he had relationships with, they spoke out about their affairs, and it helped me to make my decision. So, to you thank you for openly sharing you were the other woman. And was on a plan to destroy our union. And it worked as we both have moved on with our lives.

The ironic part of this is that he still did not marry them, he chose someone else to finish his life with. The distortion was cleared up with honesty and choosing to be better apart.

CHAPTER 8
NEW BEGINNINGS

"For all the promises of God in him are yea, and in him Amen, unto the glory of God by us." AMP 2 Corinthians 1:20 [7]

So today is the day I sit at my laptop and begin to tell the story. I like many have gone through some good times, even some great times... but I cannot speak on those without speaking on the tough times and even downright challenging times in my life.

I learned early on that your actions and decisions paint that pathway of your life. Now I am going to share a very heart wrenching part of my journey that many do not know, well do not know the truth about, it is easy to get your own perspective of someone's life looking from the outside of the glass window without really knowing what the REAL is on the inside. The view of my choices to others was distorted and full of innuendos that were not true. Most times when people do not know your life or issues, they make something up that will best suit the depiction of you, the person they have communicated to others throughout your struggle. It makes them look good to make you look less fortunate.

We often make the mistake of judging the book by the cover without knowing the content of the material inside.

Let me begin by saying, there is nothing like being a mother, period! I know that role of motherhood all too well. Yes, I have birthed 4 beautiful children now young men and young women. I am thankful and grateful to God for choosing me to be a great part of each of their lives: Anthony, Phillip, Jonelle, and Sydney these are my gifts from God, and I love them all with every part of my being. All four are awesome children and are so unique in their own way.

Let me ask you a question before we begin with my story… *Has God ever given you a gift that you had to watch from a distance? Have you ever been promised something that did not look like it would ever happen?* I pray that you did not have to go through the strenuous pain of wonder and concern, it is like a constant wound that is taking forever to heal. The actual appearance of the wound looked healed smoothly on the outside but still broken on the inside. Let us go back to the beginning of my life experience with this gift. September 1990, I became pregnant for the 2nd time, my first born was 7 at the time. All I could think is Lord, what am I going to do with another child, I was working 2 jobs when I could and did not really have a sitter or anyone to help Anthony most days. He was the sweetest kid you ever would want to know, he listened very carefully and followed instructions, unfortunately he was a latch key kid. We were a team and working on this thing called life together. I could not imagine that I would have another child during this time but on the other hand, there was a joy that I had in knowing I was getting another chance at bringing a life into this world. Every doctor's appointment, Anthony and I attended; the anticipation grew stronger.

However, I did find myself in the later months falling short of being able to financially support myself and Anthony. There was no additional financial help, and I couldn't work 2 jobs at the time it was just too much on me and my son, so I eventually fell into hard times, lost my car, lost my apartment with trying to keep the car so I could go to work and carrying this little boy inside me with great concern of both of their welfare.

I was grateful for good health and the ability to care for my son and I it was only the grace of God that we were ok. Living away from home with 2 children I knew I needed to decide will I wing it and try to stay in Columbus or move back home with the rest of my family. I pondered and thought about it, but my mother made the decision when she showed up with a truck and helped to pack me up and bring me home.

So back to Youngstown I went, about this time I was 8 1/2 months pregnant and ready for this little man to be born. I got settled living with a family member and things got a little easier of course I had support and now I could see my new bundles father more often, oh yes, he did not live in Ohio, so all this time I was in a long distant relationship, visits were planned out and phone calls were daily. This pregnancy was not only a little stressful for me but for him as well, this was going to be his first-born child. He and his family were excited about the arrival of this bundle of joy.

So, the day comes June 13th, 1991, I am in full labor at the Hospital in Youngstown, Ohio...the baby's Father and God Father are on their way, trying to make it to the birthing, unfortunately they did not make it before he was born, but nonetheless they were still excited to meet this little big boy all10 pounds of him. He was as bright as he could be with a head full of curly hair, he was so hairy, with the meanest little face you ever saw.

He looked like he was mad at the world we interrupted his good sleeping and eating inside. His father arrives, comes in to see me, kisses me on the forehead and asks for the baby. The nurse brings him in after he is all cleaned up and he sits in the chair to hold him. I never saw him like that before he was gently holding him and asking questions about how much he weighed, checking fingers and toes waiting for him to open his eyes once he did that he was in love with this little person.

Now the nurses almost took him down though, because he began to go walk the halls while holding the baby and that was a huge NO... back then folks would run out with babies, so the walking around was not allowed. Shortly after he saw the baby, he went directly to sign the birth certificate, now I named the baby prior to him getting to the hospital, however, he being the father, disagreed with Carrington Blake... it was a strong name, but he didn't like it; we had talked it over and him naming the baby was never brought up, however, he went in and changed the name to Phillip Carrington, so here was this little guy named Phillip Carrington, he was a proud father and was full of love for him, eventually that night he and the babies God Father went back to New York, and once I was released from the hospital they came back to visit for the weekend.

So now it begins I cannot say anything but good things

about little Phillip father. He bought everything that he thought we would need for the next few weeks, then he came back and did the same thing all over again. He was incredibly supportive and supplied all that "PC" needed, yes, he has a nick name thanks to his aunt, he was known as "PC."

PC grew and I loved every minute we had with him, he was about 4 weeks old and his father wanted to take the baby for his parents and family to see, now this was quite different for me I never sent my child anywhere let alone a newborn to stay without me, he wanted to keep him for a few weeks but I quickly hesitated, he didn't have his shots yet and that was just too far for me to be apart from my son.

I reached out to my mother and explained what PC's father wanted to do and she sat me down and explained to me, it is unfortunate that he lives 3 hours away, but he is his father, and you need to let him be a father to him. PC is his son too and you need to let him keep him for a few weeks. If that is what he wants to do, he will take care of him and bring him back. I have never ever thought of such a thing, this right here had me in pieces, yet I listened and spoke with his father and agreed with tears flowing to let him go. I packed up his bag and sent him with his father and his aunt.

Boy, that was the longest few weeks of my life, but as promised he brought him home. Little did I know that this would turn into a habit. It went from a 2 week visit to a month visits he would bring him back and in 2 months he was right back to get him again. Now I would visit during the breaks sometime Me, Anthony, and PC. But that changed once I started working, I could not go as much as I did prior, I could not go for a week at a time it was far and in between now. But we worked it out, no judge, no petitions, no child support notice. We did this as adults on our own and it was working. We shared custody and split our time with PC.

I just missed him terribly when he was gone. We did this back-and-forth parenting for a few years until I moved further south of Ohio. And then the time came when we needed to make a solid decision due to circumstances out of my control. How? When and What will we do?

9 NEW BEGINNINGS, PAINFUL DECISIONS

*"God is our refuge and strength (mighty and impenetrable),
A very present and well proved help in trouble."
AMP Psalms 46:1[(8)]*

*Have you ever had so much joy and love for someone and
had to make a decision that would hurt you, but you knew
it was best?* Well, my journey continues, due to a promotion
at my job I had to relocate so I packed up the boys and went.

We were still in Ohio just an hour and half away. The three
of us were on our own there. I spoke about this in an earlier
chapter, I did not know anyone in that city and since I was
there to open 2 new cash and government distribution
locations, I did not have any help at work either. I opened
and closed everyday 6 days a week. Anthony was old enough
for school in the day and PC had to go to daycare, I found
one right around the corner from my job, so I put Anthony
there after school as well. They did not have evening care
at many daycare centers back in those days so being that
I worked alone I would take my break when the day care
center closed at 6 pick the boys up and bring them back
to work with me for the last few hours. That was Monday
through Friday, and Saturday I would just pack them up and
bring them to work with me all day. I made a makeshift bed
under the counter, put a little T.V. under there and lots of toys

for them to play with. Breakfast and lunch would be in the back-break room. It was not allowed for me to have them there, especially all day, but I did not have any other choice, I did not know anyone there and I wou d not leave them home alone. I got away with it for a while, but it posed a problem when the corporate leaders came to audit the store and they found my kids underneath the counter.

PC was so bubbly he would come out from under there as soon as he would hear me speak to a customer, running back and forth and waving that only prompted Anthony to get up and chase him. It was shortly after this audit that I received a notice that my children could no longer come into the workplace with me. I was devastated and I completely understood the new policy and request. Like many young mothers I had no baoysitter and did not know anyone to keep them for me and daycare was not meeting my needs at the time. Either I quit the job and go back to public assistance services or keep the job to care for myself and the kids.

It was a rough day I remember it like yesterday. I spoke to PC's father about the situation and immediately he said, I am coming to get him. I can keep him here and I will get him in school PC was 3 at this time. I did not know what to do if I let him go, I know I have no worries about him being cared for, the family support was giant there; however, it still was without me. I cried for weeks, and I felt like a loser, I could not care for my children, but I was trying hard to do it. Anthony ended up staying home alone in the apartment until I got home from work. I was thankful for a neighbor who saw me trying to juggle this single mom working situation. I did not see PC often due to work...I had no employees for a while and was responsible for opening and closing every day. Back home in Youngstown, I began to hear the chatter when family and church family asked where the baby was... I told them with his father, and here it begins. According to those who did not see or have any dealings with me or my children, they said I lost him, and the father took him away, or I gave him up, I abandoned him and could not keep him.

The rumor mills were working fast! And of course, they would I was just another pastor's daughter having children out of wedlock and was not able to keep one. The embarrassment and humiliation of people was enough to make me feel like a complete fool, I was upset and angry most of the time and on the defense about our situation, why? Was my question most days, I could not do enough to keep my child with me. Why did I have to share him with his father 3 hours away! This was the time I completely thought about the sacred union of being married, if he had married me, I would not have had to go through any of this trauma. Or if I would not of had a child, he would not have to go through the trauma of growing up without me. Every thought you could think ran through my mind. I want to add a disclaimer here, just letting it be known truly clear, that I never ever abandoned any of my children and left them because my family did not want to help me with them. My family didn't say no to the opportunity to keep my son, unfortunately my family wasn't as able to take on a child, my mother still had children of her own to care for she was divorced and had to work a traveling job to make her ends meet, however, PC's grandparents and father was better suited at the time to care for him, no I never gave up my rights to him and never once did we step in a courthouse for custody hearing. I was not strung out on drugs or had some ill issues and had to send my son to his father.

That decision was the hardest thing I had ever done in my life and to this day it still tops as being the hardest separation ever. Until you have had to live it, you just will not understand. let this be known for all the rumors, lies and falsities told over the decades. I know that the situation seemed out of the ordinary, and it was nothing I ever wanted to do. This short-term situation turned into his life situation. We never planned for New York to be his home. I never planned to raise my children in two separate states, never in a million years would I have ever decided or planned to do that. While in my first marriage I became a stay-at-home spouse and so it should be an easy transition to have PC come back with me. Well, it was not, I would drive to New York to get a PC to bring him to stay with me and the kids and it was not pleasant for him, on top of that he missed his dad and family in NY.

📌 I will stick a pin in right here.
Ladies or Gents please watch how someone treats your children, if the parent ignores them or has issues with them and they are just a child, you would be better not to leave them in that environment. I knew my husband did not care for my son and for me going to spend time with him. It was always a fight or issue.

With that being the case, I lost a whole decade being up close and personal with my son. That was making the rumors told earlier seem even more true. There were times I would go pick him up ride 8 hours and must take him right back because he cried the whole night he wanted his father, and rightfully so. I refuse to keep him where he did not feel secure loved or wanted, So I left him there with his father and he grew to be a fine young man! He began questions in his teens wanting to know why I did not keep him with me, and I kept his siblings. He began to ask about timelines of relationships and how he felt about me not being there with him.

I explained as much as I could to him and that I never stopped loving him and caring for him. It was my duty as a mother to make sure he was in the best of care without me being there. I chose to do what was best for my child regardless of what I wanted so badly. After all the hard conversations our relationship began to rekindle at a different level. I could see him more often now. When I left Southern, Ohio, things began to turn around for me and PC. He began to visit me more often when I was able to go spend time with him in New York. When he got his driver's license and a car, he would come down to stay with us for weekends. He and his siblings-built bonds that are unbreakable, I am glad I listened and let him go, one of my promises, he was mine but far out of reach.

Once he was grown and began his singing ministry and recording endeavors it was so clear to me why he was there and why I could not leave him to be with just anyone. It was clearly purpose and an opportunity for God to show me he does keep his promises. I prayed for PC not to hate me or resent me for letting him live in New York. I did not know the pressure he had to endure watching his cousins with both of their parents, or me not being able to come at the drop of a phone call. I had to watch my promise from a distance.

I missed many days and nights when he needed his mother, but I am so grateful to his grandmother, grandfather, and his father for being there for him and raising him in the fear of the Lord, like I stated earlier I was concern with my sons feelings for me, I wanted nothing more than to know that he did love me and knew I was his mother, God is so faithful and so mindful of us his children, he didn't forget me, after all the hell I had gone through in my life it never erased the love and promise I had, and in March of 2017, I found out that God can and will keep his promise.

We came full circle, and I was given the opportunity to live with my child once again. I chose to leave Ohio and go support my child in Georgia, with the blessings of his siblings, and in 3 and a half years it was as if we were never apart. I am overwhelmed with gratefulness, and humbled that the Lord was able to place me right back to be there for him when he most needed me.

We were fully RESTORED! He is a blessing and anointed to minister to people all over the world, he is an internationally known, a Stellar Award winning and Dove Award Nominated, songwriter and recording gospel artist, spreading the word of God to everyone through his voice. I remember the day he called me he was about 13, he said mom, can I sing? I laughed on the phone and told him yes you can, at that point I shared with him about my father and the Jackson family, he responded like wow okay I did not know that. I just smiled from ear to ear because I knew it was part of his life.

Carrington Gaines name is known throughout the world, I have had people say to him to tell me, his mother, thank you for not aborting him! That comment hit deeper than many even knew because of the pain I endured from the 2 that I did abort. God can still use the rough places of our lives to bless the lives of others. For this I am profoundly grateful.

To my heartbeats Anthony, Jonelle, and Sydney, thank you for pushing me to go with your brother, I remember your words clearly, *"We have had you our entire lives, he has not, it is time."* Your unselfish love for both him and I was expressed on that day like never before.

I am forever grateful.

CHAPTER
10 THE PROBLEM WITH HAIR

"I can do all things through Christ which strengthens me"
Philippians 4:13 [9]

I know this is a turn in the direction of the story, I spoke of hair earlier in the book, however the reason I am back to it is this is the timeline in which this part took place in my journey this is the timeline in which the problem became real for me. The distorted view of me, my insecurities and why? All throughout the story of my life you heard me speaking of my hair in small doses. Let me tell you fully what inspired me to write any of this in the first place. Our bodies have a way of reacting to every emotion that we have whether it is positive or negative, traumatic, or devastating we do some damage to our bodies when we try to cover up, I have lived a life of covering and hiding so long that I cannot even stand it anymore. Those of us who have grown up in church or a strict religious family or background tend to live in an Aire of if it does not look good act like it does!

I have lived a life of my hidden truths if you will. Hiding areas of my life so deep that I even forgot some things until later in life triggers brought it back to the fore front of my mind. The very time and energy in making things look as if they are ok when they are not enough to give anyone some type of mental instability. What is so funny to me is that there were many people in my life that knew me and knew something must have been going on with me and my hair.

Especially since I went into a constant season of wigs and weave.

I remember the day sitting in the salon and I saw myself for real. The weave that was on my head and hair was pulled out! That was the hair I had left on my head, and I swelled up on the inside wailing at this great loss... I had no choice after every treatment and solution to get it to fill back in, it was completely gone and I was hurt, devastated, and embarrassed.

What was I going to do? How would I ever be able to be seen in a salon again? I did not know how I could do any of that, so the new normal began, I covered up as much as I could and lived as if it was normal. I have gone through many styles to find what fits me, some were good, a lot were not! Lol. I can laugh now about it and can finally talk freely about it.

There was a big phase of going natural with the woman of color and doing the big chop to get rid of any perm that they might have had in their hair. We were going back to our roots of wash dry; braids, plates and knots were becoming more popular. Finding our natural hair curl and being proud to wear it. I would sit and hear woman that did the big chop say: I am bald headed! It would make me cringe in my seat, often I would want to say so loud, do you want to see what bald headed is? It was nothing like my head. I was wishing to have a short nappy afro. The derogatory comments about women with truly short hair or no hair at all would hurt me to the core. I would hear the comments, watch the laughs, and feel the pain for the one they were talking about. I was no less or an exception than any other woman, so I do what I must, and hide behind the opinions of what others would say? Especially black women!

I said it we are our worst critics; we will look at a woman without hair or any lack of visually attractiveness, too fat, too short, too skinny, thin hair, really nappy hair, dry and brittle hair, big feet, big butt, giant breast and the list could go on for hours, we make a quick meme about it or send a quick post about she needs to cover her head! Not knowing the shame and inferior feeling, we are continuing to dump on the woman in question. I had over 25 years of opinions and insecurities on my shoulders, and it took me that long to know that I am beautiful with or without it, that I do not care what people say to me about my lack of mane or my piled-on wigs!

I just stopped caring about them and began to care about me. I made sure to cover my imperfection, to cover my loss to keep everyone around me comfortable with not seeing it. With not seeing the real me! And it began to take a toll on me physically and I had a decision to make. June 25th, 2022, I decided to go into a barber shop and have my head looked at with no hair and ask for this man cut weave, or hair replacement option to cover what needed covering and cut as low as I can get it. Now the barber I used is a total angel and has a gift from God. Her name is Valyn "Queen of Fades" Benson. I was searching all the major cities to see where I could go to get this procedure done. When I was advised that there is someone in the area who can help me.

I swallowed my fear and reached out to her. And today I am

so glad I did. Now because I have lost most all my hair due to traction alopecia, stress, and medication, I opted to try this option, hair replacement, it was the closest thing to me being able to have my hair blended into the weave added. Not every barber or stylist can do this certain procedure. I opened myself up and was vulnerable finally.

I told no one when and what I was going to do with my hair for my birthday, not even my family, I just did it! And showed up like here I am. Surprisingly the responses were mostly positive of course I got some negative remarks, even as bad as asking if I was gay! All because I changed my look. I was ok with the remarks because I finally opened my mouth and said you do not have to like it, I do! And it is none of your business why I cut it this way.

We are a very judgmental people and do not always think before we speak, I am glad I was strong enough to handle the stares comments and whatever else they threw at me that only came from me being fed up with trying to please everyone else for so many years. So now I am at the I do not care era in my life. I like hair and I will always have some type of style on my head ... but the day is nearing where I totally am open to wearing absolutely nothing on my head in public!

That will be the final milestone for me with this head of mine. Just know I will change it up in a minute hair, no hair, whatever I feel. What I realized about my view of myself, is it was dependent on looks, if I did not have a certain look no one would like me, if I did not have hair everyone would talk bad about me, I was so worried about others that I now had a superficial view of myself. I did not even love my own self because others may not like the self I truly was. It was a distorted view. I hated what was happening to me and I did not know how to see me past it.

So, for decades I walked around like someone else. Someone I wished I could be. I listened to many conversations about women with my condition and it was always a laughing joke or derogative comments that described the person. I did not want to fall into that group of being laughed at and spoken of in a derogative way. What I finally faced after all these years God has preserved me and kept me, he knows the very count of hairs that I lost many years ago, he knows that I do not have all I started out with, but he still loves me and cares for me. If only I could have captured this, then I would not have had to walk around with the mask of shame for twenty plus years. I am not defined by the hair on my head, and I am not defined by the lack thereof. I am beautiful and I am free to speak about my truth. I am sure some will say well why do you still wear wigs or weave? I do it because I like it, I like hair and cosmetology has evolved so we can wear whatever we want to know, however you want. So, I may choose to put a wig on or weave it out just depending on how I feel. If I choose not to do either that is fine too because I love me either way. I am me and I finally see me for who I am. Past the comments and past the shame of loss, I am a real person with real feelings, and I respect everyone's opinions but will not cover up to help you deal with my imperfections or loss. I no longer will inconvenience myself to make it comfortable for those will talk about it or me later, so my thought is get used to it.

The new Bald Beauty. The distorted view of who I am is no longer the measure by which I see myself and place myself in any status. I am ME! I Lost everything over the past 30 years at the expense of others who did not care to see the damage formulating on me day after day and now I win because of the losses, I say wining because it forced me to see the real me, it forced me to remove the insecurity of letting others know I was hurt and suffering in silence.
We no longer do that. Help is here no matter if you are young old or in-between, you have a right to be happy, secure and confident in your own skin. The only way that this happened to me is when I was finally true to myself.

You cannot love what you always hide.

CHAPTER
11 A TRUE FRIEND

"Two are better than one, because they have a good reward for their labor" AMP Ecclesiastes 4:9 (10)

The divorces are over, and my children are all grown, I go through a decade of trying to reinvent myself, I am no longer anyone's wife and no longer associated with any male. It is just me. I found out that I would be ok without a husband. I found out that I can take care of myself, but I had to learn to appreciate my new self. I did not have a lot of friends. I shut that out after knowing what friends did for my mom and myself. I had an exceedingly small circle.

I thank God for relationships and the friends that I truly have, God will never leave you alone, he will send you relationships to help build you in the stages of life that you are in. Everyone needs someone that they can totally be transparent with, and the Lord sent me just that. Someone who did not judge me, or my financial status, someone who really cared about my being and someone that would cuss me out if I said or did the wrong thing, I never knew that I could be friends with someone so opposite of me, but that Is exactly what I needed. I remember the first time I was able to share my true feelings and thoughts about myself and they never judged me, and never repeated it.

I remember the day I finally showed my little bald head, and they never said a negative word, just always full of inspiration and compliments. You know it is a loyal friend when they say ok let us see a professional about this, always offered help and never asked for anything in return.

When I was sick or not feeling well, they were there to help, when I felt like a failure, they were there to lift me up, I was able to see what I had missed in all the years of my life, FRIENDSHIP! I will be honest having friends was not on the top of my list at all. I watched my mother be devastated from a girlfriend and I refused to allow that to happen to me. But I really needed a friend, someone to keep it real with me and be my honest self. It changed my life and view of what a friend was to be.

I thank God for my Sister Friend Marnie she never knew that me helping her with what she needed was helping me to deal with the trauma I was facing I call her sister because she knows me just like a sister and never ever judges me on my transparency. When I had to start over again, she was right there while going through divorce she was right there for me. And has never changed, I believe that God places people in our lives according to the need in our lives and she showed me that I could trust again, and I could have friends.

Throughout my divorce and on my own journey I went through a series of always trying to find a home to suit everyone else, making room for everyone else. I moved 4 times after my last divorce, that was surprising, going from a homeowner to trying to rent was horrific.

I had my mother and the girls again for a while and was

always trying to accommodate them and not myself, rent
I could not afford and space that was too much for me at the
time. I have lived my life to please others always and never
for myself that left me in financial ruins.

I remember when I moved to MY first apartment just for me!
That was 2015, I was so excited I loved my place it was out
of the way, and out of the city limits it was perfect, there is
where I found out that I like being at home alone and I love
having movie night every Friday, I would rent movies order
my pizza and wings and enjoy movies at home. Now because
I loved this freedom of living with just me for a change, it did
not remove the fact that I wished I had someone to watch a
movie with, someone to talk to and have date night. I know
that I cannot stay in this era of singleness for the rest of my
days or rather I desire not to because I would like to have a
companion someone to grow old with.

Someone to experience true love, respect and commitment
to each other, no outside interference. I learned from my
friends that I can have fun and trust my friends to be there
for me. It does not make me a sinner because I interact
with those outside of my faith. I lived a sheltered life and
listened to a lot of people advising what I could and could
not do in my life. Which resulted in me not knowing anything
personally about me, when asked what you like to do? I
could not even answer because I really did not know, it
took me finally branching out and learning to do other stuff
outside of children and others' opinions... I was a mother and
a wife all my life from the age of 16 and that is all I knew.

So, I began to branch out and do things for myself. Some

of my favorites with my friends were long rides out in the middle of nowhere, eating authentic Italian food till I was about to burst. I loved the me that I was becoming. I love taking risks, loving myself and being content with myself.

Taking one tank trips for myself celebrating my birthday by myself! It was all a part of making me who I am today. For me to truly see that I was perfect the way that I was I had to endure all the hardship and traumatic events ...like a true diamond I was buried in mess covered and needed everything horrible, burned off to see the shine God has on my life. I am finally at a place of true love for me. I have failed in relationships prior, maybe if I knew then what I know now I may have been able to salvage the relationship. Maybe! not, however.

I am grateful for the test and trials in my life, if I can help someone else see that they too are valuable and worth all God has for them. I desire to inspire women like me all over the world. I want to be a springboard to help others regain their self-esteem and self-worth. I read in the word of God, that he came to give us life and life more abundantly, so our lives are not to be one dimensional but to be well rounded emotionally, physically, socially, and spiritually.

I am a better person after losing. Do I wish I had my hair hanging down my back again? Yes, do I wish I had my family and husband back? Sometimes, but not really because I desire to know what it is like to have someone love me for the real person I am today. I found out I do not need what I use to have to be what God has created me to be.
I see me and I love it.

12 WHAT KIND OF LOVE IS THIS

"You shall not witness falsely against your neighbor"
AMP Exodus 20 :16 [11]

I am not sure who needs to hear this part, but I pray the right person does. With today's way of living family dynamics are so different than when I grew up.

I am grateful to God for every trial every let down and every battle of disappointment. I have endured various areas of pain in my life that should have taken me out of here. I really should have been crazy by now, yes literally insane, but God, despite people and their made-up stories as to why and all the laughs and looks about me being bald headed and all the laughs about me being the going joke in town because my husband weren't faithful, and how many times I was married, and it must be me as to why it didn't work out... After all that my self-esteem was not even existent, I had none.

I felt less than for most of my life, trying to be a good person, trying to look the part for the church's sake. All of this has had me so heavy.

All my life never being enough and holding on to the traumatic actions that took place in my life as a child. I finally think about it and pray lord the next one will love me for me, he will want me and not want to just have sex with me, he will want me for life. Flaws and all... One final episode put the nail in the coffin for me.

After years of love lost, I find myself back in Ohio from Georgia to care for my mother and love shows up at my door again... I meet a man who is saying all the right things and doing all the right things he loves God and is serious about kingdom work. We met and it was fast moving in the 6 months he surprised me with a whole lip sync performance, it was a Sunday and after his church service. He came out in this costume and began to lip sing Real Love. I am not looking at him, I thought it was part of the show they were doing at the church and I look up because everyone is laughing and gathering around, and he is singing to me, now the words to the song said I'm looking for a real love, I realize this is all about me, he brings a cake over and gets on one knee and says I never want to live without you, will you be my wife for the rest of my life?

I was in shock, and the emotions took over, I was completely in awe! Let me give you a little history of our journey, despite all the things I had dealt with in the past he did not care. He introduced me to the family, and I loved them, I got caught up in the kindness and willingness to be there for me, but it was in a whirl wind. He says to me in the beginning we will not have sex until after marriage because he wants the Lord to bless it. However, a year into the engagement unforeseen things happen and dishonesty is uncovered. He was not the man I thought he was, and because I have not and will not disclose his flaws publicly, I will say that it is especially important to know who you are in relationship with, dating in your fifties is nothing like dating at the age of twenties. You must ask questions and never remove the feeling of doubt or the not sure about a person.

He wanted to move quickly to get married and I kept saying no. It would be all right to wait.

He had no intention of telling me the truth about himself, issues physically, his preferences intimately, along with his financial status and health, until after the wedding, and he made sure to tell me a few times we will not have intercourse until we get to the honeymoon. So strange after you have waited all this time who would not on their honeymoon night. However, God never leaves me without a warning, and I am too old to ignore the warning signs just to have someone.

I have learned through past mistakes to take heed and ask questions, now at this point save the dates have been mailed, bridesmaid dresses are bought, and I have a whole gown still hanging on my door in my bedroom. I chose not to accept less than what I know God has for me. There are those who will creep IN and the next thing you know you are stuck in a marriage of deceit and lies.

I could not do it to save face. I let it go and called the whole thing off. How embarrassing and degrading I felt. I shut myself up for a while, cried a bit and prayed until it turned into thank you lord for saving me moments. After telling everyone what happened I found myself angry and mad about something I had not felt before. I talked to my sisters and friends, and it still did not help. I was heading down after this. I was downright mad and wanted nothing to do with church, or people, I could not understand why this was happening to me. I was forthcoming and discussed what we should at this point, but I heard the voice of my Pastor when he said to me, if somebody wants to trick you, they will trick you! How would I know I was headed into a trap of deceit again? So, I took the embarrassment and let all who needed to know it was not my final time in love.

This made me feel a horrible way, and I began to blame myself and thought I would not be able to trust anyone! It was so heavy on me that I finally got to the place where I needed some help and not help from the church, the pastors or anyone else... I finally at 54 decided I needed to talk to someone outside of my circle. I found a licensed therapist, and I allowed myself to be open and honest about my whole life.

I started going through therapy and it was the best thing I have done in my life outside of saying yes, the Jesus Christ. I met with her weekly as I progressed throughout a year with her, I am not ashamed to say I needed someone to help me understand me! I was in a bad mental and emotional state and so I was available for me; to unpack 54 years of trauma, to unpack 54 years of lack of love, trust, and commitment. It started with me being devastated over this last attempt at love, but found it was not this last attempt at love at all, it had been a lifelong event of lost love and trauma that had me in this angry and mad state. I always found myself so busy helping others but never thought to help myself. I open my eyes so I can see that I am exactly who he created me to be.

I am a great mother, and a loving sister, and an even better daughter having gone through this life. Women have it hard sometimes; we must make tough decisions that will affect our whole lives, we sometime accept what someone wants to give us instead of waiting it out for what we are worth. Sexual abuse, mental and physical abuse, verbal abuse, they all take a toll on us, and we take on the garment of the abuser or the mistakes that we have made in our lives. I thank God for this woman I had no idea about, she did not know me, and I did not know her, she helped me to see why I was so accepting and such a magnet to rejection, hurt and abuse from people.

I was always trying to be good! Do the right thing to help others hide the abuse hurt that they caused in my life. The truth is I refused to admit to the hurt, the failure and to the fact I was not helping myself by being quiet and accepting what was done to me, I accepted the men in my life, and their way of living with unfaithfulness and deceit, this came from a low self-esteem and low view of myself. This therapist helped me unpack my life and if it were not for her, I never would have been able to see the real me, I was losing myself because of the pressure of hiding was crushing my very being.

If I could be an example to every woman in this world, please let me be that. We can overcome our fears, our failures and even our mistakes, but we must first uncover it. Speak what you feel and refuse the negative remarks looks and stares. You matter, and your voice matters, this is important. Know yourself and know your worth. The thought of seeking some psychological help was never a plan for me, however, going through the exercises and doing the homework assigned to me is the reason I have the boldness to speak my truth now, it was a process to meet the real me and now try to help someone else who battles with the same issues.

Some would say why would you want to marry again after two failed marriages? I will be honest, when I look at who I am, not the position of and Elder in my church, but myself as a woman. I do not want to have a boyfriend coming in and out of my life, I know that the desire for physical touch and desired intimacy is a real thing, and I am not ok with hooking up as the young people say, just to hook up.

What I possess is more than a hook up or fast-food service, quickly visit when you want to and leave with my goods. No, I want a tangible full fledge love relationship with the right man for me, the man who will know all of what I have experienced throughout my life.

He will show me what real love and commitment is. So, until he who God has for me comes, I will be single waiting and working until he (HIM) crosses my path.

I urge all of you reading this book right now to allow yourself the opportunity of freedom, it is okay to seek some help and unpack the baggage you hide.

These few chapters are just a quick overview of my life, an introduction if you will, for women to come out of hiding. It is not super spiritual, extra deep and wonderful, it is simply a good old fashion reality. This is my reality. My reality is all God wanted me to see. It was all he wanted me to reveal so I could be healed. **I went through hiding it when all God wanted was to use it for his Glory. My Truth.**

CHAPTER 13 NEW IMAGE MINISTRY

"Do not (earnestly) remember the former things; neither consider the things of old." AMP Isaiah 43:18 [12]

After going through the traumatic loss of my hair and covering up my imperfections I have come to a place of transparency, and no longer want to hide who I am, but share who and what I have gone through. There are many women in this world who suffer the same loss as I do with balding, alopecia, or traction alopecia. However, it may have come about because of stresses through life, or it could be hereditary.

Whatever the reason it can be embarrassing and isolating and can leave a negative influence on your self-esteem. Please know that you do not have to suffer in silence, New Image Ministry is a non-profit organization for Women, not excluding men and children who suffer with hair loss and the effects from it that may alter your lives. In a world full of beauty and numerous ways to enhance your look with wigs, weave, or implants, some may not want to accept societies' views of beauty trends. Some may want to simply Uncover and be viewed as a beautiful person with or without the latest styles or longest locks. This ministry came about as I accepted my own truth, I do not want another woman to go through life feeling as though she is less of a woman or not beautiful because of the lack of hair, the lack of confidence and self-love. I am reassuring the women of all ethnicities to come out of the hiding and the shame placed on us through society's way of thinking or acceptance.

Our Goal at New Image Ministry is to build others up and help in the way we can help achieve the style look and replacement of hair that would suit the individual. Let us build up what may have been the greatest let down you have suffered.

Please visit my social media platform on Facebook
New Image Ministry

For bookings, donations or information contact me
Uncover@newimageministry.com
Linktr.ee/cherellepwardjackson
Phone: 330-333-9464

TESTIMONIALS

As a young girl gazing at that beautiful smile with large, gorgeous dimples, the excitement in your eyes at no longer having to monitor your younger siblings was as if they were your own. Oh, what a joy it was to be a teenager, to spend a little time with your peers before becoming a teenage mother, and then life began. You had undeniable joy! I observed from near and far, and you held your head high for the HOLIER THAN THOU PEOPLE. You know, the individuals who whispered and acted as if they had never done anything; they simply never shown how they were forced to marry or how their parents reared their children. Yet, I saw the agony and suffering and wished to alleviate it all, but I could not beat up everyone who had harmed you, could I?

But I saw you get stronger, and you kept progressing. After the birth of your second son, things became more difficult; you worked so hard and even took him to work with you and had him under your desk, but you had no assistance, and it was only temporary. The anguish, the gnawing, the ache, and the sense of yet another loss grew out of the fragmented remnants of childhood trauma and previous relationships. You moved on, put on a STRONG FACE, and acted like everything was fine, but you never lived in YOUR REAL TRUTH. But then, Marriage No.1 occurs. Son of a pastor, I assumed he was a man of God. You wore that title well, dressed appropriately, and smiled despite the devastation. Your offspring were fortunate because you shielded them from all knowledge. The anguish, the trauma, the brokenness, and the pain. You had to grow because of your experiences. Nevertheless, you grew through the season you *were in, just enough to begin again. You buried your guilt, shame, hurt, and anguish and convinced yourself you were prepared. But now you have probed deep and discovered assistance along the way, healing from the inside out, knowing who you are, whose you are, and VALUING YOURSELF. Now, having the opportunity to witness you living in an honest manner is a priceless gift. After there has been a realignment and the eyesight has been rectified using the COMPLETE VIEW (Truth from the inward and The Father's Plan), your distorted perspective will be useful in bringing clarity to the views of others. Nevertheless, it is during these junctures of our journey that our viewpoint, or the bits of it that have been scattered here and there, join to make a MASTERPIECE. Continue advancing in your life and achieving everything God has planned for you.*

STAY LIBERATED AND LIVE IN TRUTH!

Your Sister,
~ Darla J White MA, MAPCC, MTh.

I cannot label my relationship with Cherelle as 'FRIENDSHIP' because it is more than that. Much more! It is a relationship with my SOUL that I hope everyone is Blessed to experience in their lifetime. The moment I met her, my body and soul became overwhelmed with joy, love, tears, and a feeling I had never felt before. I knew it was our souls connecting and welcoming each other. I knew then that this bond would be for a LIFETIME. My love and faith for God began to FLOURISH more than ever. I learned to love myself and who I was. My hate was diminished and my love for others grew and grew. She taught me to pray and pray faithfully. To give it to God and mean it. In addition, we shared our life stories. Our joys and our sadness, our trials, and tribulations, without judgment. I often wondered, how could this person who was BROKEN like me, have the empathy and love to encourage me. I will tell you how, Her Faith in God and her willingness to never give up or go back, her courage to author this book and put it into words. Her setbacks and forthcomings. I thank God every day for Cherelle, and I hope that everyone reading this gets the chance to meet their soul sister or brother.

Your Sister,
~ Marnie J. Martini

To give a few words about the wonderful author of this memoir, Distorted View is a complicated task, such an amazing force and so many things that can be said and mentioned about experiencing her.

The first initial times of meeting the wonderful Cherelle were throughout the second half of my high school career from her daughter, my best friend Jonelle. From interactions at school events, home visits and church attending after a while she and her surrounding family were like another family to me.

From leaving high school to moving into college and staying with her and the family, the interactions I have experienced with her were always considerate, sincere, and willing even in times of hardships from life occurrences.

To things and events happening in my life over time as well as understanding that life was also happening for those surrounding me, there was never any exclusions of how much she would always extend herself to do what she could to ensure others, myself included as well as her own were okay.

To know and to experience the wonderful connection and genuine consideration of Mama Relle is to know that no matter what or how, she is sure to be as pure and as compassionate as ever. The ways that she is there to connect and assist her family is the same way and have the same support and will, as she would have for anyone, she truly felt she just needed a helping hand. The way she loves and the ways that she follows the lord, and his words truly express the true gift she is to the world. To know her is to love her and the way that she loves people, she takes no mess but is always fair and becoming an additional daughter is an honor. Partaking in the journey of this book will guarantee her joy and light to shine on the pages as bright as she lights up any room she enters. I want to thank you from the bottom of my heart for everything you have ever done for me and everyone else out there, Congratulations!

With all the love to send,
~ Charidan H.

ABOUT
THE AUTHOR

My parents named me Cherelle Patrice Jackson, I am a mother of 4 beautiful children, and 4 beautiful bonus children as well as a grandmother of 17 and one on the way. I have a bachelor's degree in Christian Theology, and I am an Ordained Elder in Ministry. I have a deep passion for ministry, community, and wellbeing of others especially women and children.

My life has had a great deal of unexpected situations and circumstances, but not totally void of some joys, fulfillments, and love. I am grateful to share it with you today, not every day is perfect and often times we get stuck in the not so perfect times and to keep the outside world from knowing what is happening inside we develop a mask of hope and perfection that we, or I believed, was necessary to protect myself, my family members and my reputation within the church and community.

Living my False Truth was as normal to me as getting up and getting dressed each day. The reality of it is before I walked out of my door, I made sure to put my mask on. The mask that hid me from me, along with the mask to hide the real me from others. I lived it and I can speak from experience you will become weary and void of your worth and purpose. I pray that my transparency will allow you to see just a portion of me and my journey to wholeness. I want to encourage you to speak out, be honest, and get help. I am a witness that you can be free, and you too can be free.

Go live your truth! Uncover Heal Transform

~ Cherelle Patrice Ward

ACKNOWLEDGMENTS

First, I thank God for his mercy and grace! I thank him for giving me the strength to share my TRUTH.

I want to thank my children for all their support and love. You pushed me, held me up and prayed for me. I love you all for life, thank you to my mother and Father (RIH) love you Dad, Phyllis P. Jackson, and my family, I love you all, we are the Jacksons!

This book could not have become known without the help of my Therapist Ms. L. Prince, thank you for all your expertise, patience, and care, pulling me out of me.

Also, to Valyn (Queen of Fades) Benson, you accepted my call without hesitation, and offered service to me with dignity, security, and privacy. Thank you for allowing me to see what I thought would only be on my Wish list. You are the coldest barber I ever had! Thank you for making it happen every time.

To Gooch! The Professional Master Stylist/ Man of God! You put the icing on the cake. I came for a pixie look and left with a whole message from God, thank you for being used by God and for being a friend of over 25 years, I appreciate and love you more than you will know.

For my Glam team my daughters, THANK YOU!
MUA Sydney C. McIntyre; (Pretty with Sydney) Nail Artist;
Janae Ward (Nails by Nae) and Charie E. You are the greatest.

For the beautiful Photos, a great big Thank you to On Sight Photography and More in Youngstown, Ohio, your professionalism and attention to detail and keen eye made me look GREAT!

I want to give a special thanks to my church family, Christ Centered Church, and Bishop Kenneth W. Paramore for being that father in ministry I needed, you listened, you guided and supported as fathers do! I am forever grateful for the push parents give to eaglets in the nest. You pushed me but not before time, but right on time. Great blessings, favor and love to you and Pastor Leta Paramore forever.

To my manuscript and publishing coach Mrs. Gail E. Dudley, you are the truth! Thank you is not enough. I appreciate all your help, leadership, and support.

Finally, to my sisters and God sisters, Kimberly, Darla, and Melissa & Claretta (watching over us) Michelle you were there all the time to support, listen and love thank you I cannot express in words my love for you.

To My Tribe Sister –friends!
I love you all, Thank you for your support.

~ C. Patrice

CITING

"I will confess and praise You, for You are fearful and wonderful; and for the awful wonder of my birth!"

The Amplified Bible Copyright 1954, 1958, 1962, 1965,1987 by
The Lockman Foundation AMP Zondervan I Psalms 139:14a (1)

"But if a woman has long hair, it is her ornament and glory? for her hair is given to her for a covering."

The Amplified Bible Copyright 1954, 1958, 1962, 1965,1987 by
The Lockman Foundation AMP Zondervan I AMP 1 Corinthians 11:15 (2)

"You shall not commit adultery"

The Amplified Bible Copyright 1954, 1958, 1962, 1965,1987 by
The Lockman Foundation AMP Zondervan I AMP Exodus 20:14 (3)

"For all that is in the world, the lust of the flesh, and the lust of the eyes, and the pride of life, is not of the Father, but is of the world."

The Amplified Bible Copyright 1954, 1958, 1962, 1965,1987 by
The Lockman Foundation AMP Zondervan I AMP 1 John 2:16 (4)

"Let marriage be held in honor (esteemed worthy, precious, of great price, and especially dear) in all things."

The Amplified Bible Copyright 1954, 1958, 1962, 1965,1987 by
The Lockman Foundation AMP Zondervan I AMP Hebrews 13:4 AMP (5)

"Husbands love your wives, as Christ love the church and gave Himself up for her."

AMP Ephesians 5:25 (6)

"For all the promises of God in him are yes, and in him Amen, unto the glory of God by us."

"God is our refuge and strength, A very present help in trouble."

"I can do all things through Christ which strengthens me"

"Two are better than one, because they have a good reward for their labor."

"You shall not witness falsely against your neighbor."

"Do not (earnestly) remember the former things; neither consider the things of old."

What's your

DISTORTED VIEW ?

**Here's space and opportunity
for you to write your story**

www.ingramcontent.com/pod-product-compliance
Lightning Source LLC
Chambersburg PA
CBHW060529130626
46553CB00002B/690